UNICORN FOOD

UNICORN FOOD

RAINBOW TREATS AND COLORFUL CREATIONS TO ENJOY AND ADMIRE

CAYLA GALLAGHER

HOST OF THE YouTube COOKING SHOW, PANKOBUNNY

Skyhorse Publishing

Skyhorse Publishing books may be purchased in bulk at special discounts for sales promotion, corporate gifts, fund-raising, or educational purposes. Special editions can also be created to specifications. For details, contact the Special Sales Department, Skyhorse Publishing, 307 West 36th Street, 11th Floor, New York, NY 10018 or info@skyhorsepublishing.com.

Skyhorse® and Skyhorse Publishing® are registered trademarks of Skyhorse Publishing, Inc.®, a Delaware corporation.

Visit our website at www.skyhorsepublishing.com.

10 9 8 7 6 5 4 3 2

Library of Congress Cataloging-in-Publication Data

Names: Gallagher, Cayla, author.
Title: Unicorn food : rainbow treats and colorful creations to enjoy and
    admire / by Cayla Gallagher.
Description: New York, NY : Skyhorse Publishing, [2018]
Identifiers: LCCN 2017055676| ISBN 9781510732353 (hardcover: alk. paper) |
    ISBN 9781510732377 (ebook)
Subjects: LCSH: Cake. | Cookies. | Desserts. | LCGFT: Cookbooks.
Classification: LCC TX771 .G35 2018 | DDC 641.86—dc23 LC record available
    at https://lccn.loc.gov/2017055676

Cover design by Jenny Zemanek
Cover photograph by Cayla Gallagher

Print ISBN: 978-1-5107-3235-3
Ebook ISBN: 978-1-5107-3237-7

Printed in China

Contents

INTRODUCTION

When I was first contacted about writing a cookbook, I was floored! Never in my wildest dreams did I think I would have the opportunity to write a cookbook only three years into my career. I'm not going to lie, there were happy tears and celebratory dancing involved! I am so excited to be able to provide you with my favorite, tried-and-true recipes and the fun unicorn touches I've added to them! These recipes are solid—follow the steps and they'll work out every single time. They're also designed to be customized by you! I want to share with you the skills that I've learned from hosting my YouTube channel these last four years: that all recipes can be tweaked to suit your personal preference, the seasons, or an event! Be creative and take risks—try stuffing the RAINBOW FRENCH TOAST (page 151) with a completely different filling (chocolate and raspberries would be divine!), or add different spices or flavorings to turn the RAINBOW NO-CHURN ICE CREAM (page 133) into your own custom flavor. I have done several variations of the UNICORN FUDGE (page 171) on my YouTube channel, and each version began by seeing a different ingredient and wondering how it would taste in fudge. And I've got to say, each version is always better than the last! The recipes in this book were all developed the same way: by embracing creativity and having a relentless sweet tooth.

This cookbook is a culmination of several goals I had when I started my YouTube channel. The first was to show people how to transform everyday food into works of art, or what I call "edible cuteness." I found by making simple tweaks, like adding food coloring or carving a cake in an unusual way, I could completely change a recipe and elevate it to an entirely new level. Food is such a personal, sentimental part of life, so I loved the idea of playing around with traditional recipes and creating new experiences for my readers.

The original, non-unicorn version of the UNICORN BANANA BREAD recipe in this book (page 165) is a family favorite, and quite honestly, my mom will always make it better than I can. I used to come home after school to warm muffins in my kitchen. As I've gotten older, those muffins have become comfort food that I make for myself, friends, and boyfriends. I was delighted when I had the opportunity to share this family favorite on my YouTube channel and subscribers began sending me photos of their own personal recreations.

This brings me to the second goal this book has helped me to achieve; having the incredible privilege of joining my readers and subscribers in their kitchens and helping them create dishes to celebrate events and milestones in their own lives, and most importantly, create memories with their loved ones. There is no greater joy than receiving a photo or video from a subscriber of a recipe that they recreated and hearing how it tasted good and was such a success. Every time I receive a photo, I'm always reminded of why I do what I do and this makes me so ridiculously happy. I love that I can contribute even the tiniest bit of light or happiness to my viewers' lives, and please, if you try out any of the recipes in this book, send me a photo on Twitter or Instagram @pankobunny—I would love to see your creations!

I want to sincerely thank each and every one of you for purchasing this book and for supporting my brand and YouTube channel, pankobunny. I am able to live my dream because of your support, and I hope that this cookbook is everything you hoped it would be!

—Love,
Cayla

CAKES

Vanilla Confetti Cake

This beautiful cake is the perfect colorful birthday cake, with sprinkles inside and out! Learn a fun technique on how to coat the cake in sprinkles—it's much easier than you'd expect!

Cake batter:

1 cup unsalted butter, room temperature
2 cups sugar
2 tsp. vanilla extract
6 large eggs, room temperature
3 cups all-purpose flour
1 tsp. baking soda
1 tsp. salt
1¼ cups sour cream
1 cup confetti sprinkles

Vanilla buttercream:

2 cups unsalted butter, room temperature
1 tsp. vanilla extract
5 cups confectioner's sugar
3 cups confetti sprinkles

Bake the cake:

1. Preheat the oven to 350°F.

2. Place the butter and sugar in a bowl and beat with an electric mixer until pale and fluffy. Add the vanilla, then the eggs one at a time, mixing with each addition.

3. In a separate bowl, mix together the flour, baking soda, and salt. Add this to the butter mixture in 2 additions, alternating with the sour cream. Add the confetti sprinkles and mix to combine.

4. Divide the batter between 2 greased and floured 9-inch round cake pans and bake for 25–30 minutes, or until a skewer inserted into the cakes comes out clean.

5. Cool the cakes in the pan for 5 minutes, then transfer to a wire rack and cool completely.

Make the buttercream:

1. Cream the butter with an electric mixer until pale and fluffy. Add the vanilla extract and beat until combined. Add the confectioner's sugar one cup at a time, then beat for 3–5 minutes, until fluffy.

Assembly:

1. Slice the tops and bottoms off of each cake, flattening them and removing any excess browning. Place a cake board on top of each cake and trim off the browned edges. Then slice each cake in half to create 2 layers each.

2. Place a round cake board onto your work surface and stack the 4 layers of cake on top, spreading about ½ cup buttercream between each layer. Then coat cake evenly in the remaining buttercream.

3. Place a second cake board on top of the cake. Line a cookie sheet with parchment paper and fill with the remaining 3 cups confetti sprinkles. Turn the cake on its side, with one hand on each cake board, and roll the sides of the cake in the sprinkles, until all sides are evenly covered. Return the cake to your work surface.

4. Remove the top cake board and smooth the buttercream, if it has shifted. Sprinkle the top with the remaining sprinkles. Enjoy!

TIP: *If you don't have cake boards on hand, simply cut out two 8" circles from a sheet of cardboard and wrap tightly in plastic wrap!*

No-Bake Rainbow Cheesecake

This beautiful cheesecake is gelatin-free and is perfect for anyone who cannot consume pork (as this product is often found in gelatin). It is a wonderfully smooth, creamy cheesecake that can be eaten with a spoon—try stopping at just one piece!

Cheesecake base:

5 tbsp. unsalted butter, melted
2⅓ cups animal crackers, crumbled into very
   small pieces

Cheesecake filling:

1¾ cups cream cheese, room temperature
6½ tbsp. sugar
1¾ cups whipping cream
¼ cup lemon juice
½ tsp. vanilla extract
Pink, orange, yellow, green, blue,
   and purple food coloring

1. First, make the base of the cheesecake. Combine the melted butter and crumbled animal crackers, then press into the bottom of an 8-inch springform pan. Place in the fridge while you make the filling.

2. To make the filling, place the cream cheese in a bowl and beat with an electric mixer until smooth. Add the sugar and combine. Add the whipping cream, lemon juice, and vanilla extract and mix until smooth. Divide the mixture into 6 bowls and dye them the colors of the rainbow, adding a couple drops of pink to the first bowl, a couple drops orange to the next, etc.

3. Pour the filling into the cake pan one color at a time, freezing for 10 minutes between each layer. This will prevent the layers from mixing together. When all the colors have been added, return the cheesecake to the freezer to set for 1–2 hours. You don't want the cheesecake to completely freeze, just to stiffen. If you'd prefer a softer cheesecake, only freeze for 1 hour.

4. Wet a dishcloth with hot water and run it around the sides of the pan to slightly warm the cake. Remove the sides of the pan, slice, and enjoy!

Gummy Bear Cake

A cake covered in gummy bears—why choose one treat when you can have both? The gummy bears glow from the bright buttercream underneath and will create a stunning centerpiece to any party!

Cake batter:

2 cups all-purpose flour
3½ tsp. baking powder
½ tsp. salt
½ cup unsalted butter, room temperature
1 cup sugar
1 tsp. vanilla extract
2 eggs
1 cup milk
¼ cup rainbow sprinkles

Vanilla buttercream:

2 cups unsalted butter, room temperature
1 tsp. vanilla extract
5 cups confectioner's sugar
Neon food coloring

Approx. 4 cups gummy bears

Bake the cake:

1. Combine the flour, baking powder, and salt in a bowl. In a separate bowl, beat the butter with an electric mixer until pale and fluffy. Add the sugar and mix until combined. Add the vanilla extract and eggs and beat until combined. Add the dry ingredients in 2 additions, alternating with the milk.

2. Add the sprinkles and mix until just combined. Divide into 2 greased 9-inch round cake pans and bake at 350°F for 20–25 minutes, or until fully cooked. Cool completely.

Make the buttercream:

1. Cream the butter with an electric mixer until pale and fluffy. Add the vanilla extract and beat until combined. Add the confectioner's sugar one cup at a time, then beat for 3–5 minutes, until fluffy.

2. Set aside half the buttercream, then divide the remaining buttercream into 3 separate bowls. Dye them any neon colors of your choice.

Assembly:

1. Cut the cakes into clean circles and trim the tops and bottoms, creating even surfaces. Slice each cake in half to create a total of 4 layers.

2. Place one layer of cake on a serving tray of your choice and spread one bowl of the neon buttercream over the entire surface. Repeat with another layer of cake and the next neon buttercream, until you reach the final layer of cake. Cover the entire surface of the cake with the white buttercream.

3. Place 2 red gummy bears at the base of the cake, followed by 2 orange, 2 yellow, 2 green, and 2 clear gummy bears. Repeat until both ends of the gummy bear chain meet. Repeat directly above the gummy bears, but shift the position slightly, so that the first red gummy bear on the second level is positioned between the two red gummy bears on the first level. Repeat until the entire cake is covered. Place more gummy bears onto the center of the cake and serve!

Surprise Crepe Cake

This cake is overflowing with candies and rainbows! The white chocolate cream filling pairs deliciously with the delicately sweet crepes and will give your guests quite a surprise when they slice into the cake and discover rainbows inside.

Crepe batter:

1¾ cups all-purpose flour
½ cup potato starch
¼ cup sugar
2½ cups milk
A few drops vanilla extract

Cream filling:

2½ cups whipping cream
¼ cup white chocolate, melted
Pink, orange, yellow, green, blue,
   and purple food coloring

Colorful candy
Yogurt-dipped pretzels
Unicorn Poop Marshmallows (page 83)

Make the crepes:

1. Place the flour, potato starch, and sugar in a bowl and lightly beat with an electric mixer. This will break up lumps and eliminates the need to sift the ingredients. Add the milk ½ cup at a time, mixing with each addition. Add the vanilla extract and mix until the batter is smooth.

2. Set a lightly greased frying pan to medium heat and pour in enough batter to just cover the bottom of the pan. Bring the heat down to low and place a lid on the pan. Cook the crepe until the surface is fully cooked, about 2–3 minutes.

3. Gently loosen the edges of the crepe from the pan using a chopstick or offset spatula, then flip the crepe out onto a plate. Transfer the crepe to a cooling rack. Continue with the remaining batter—you should be able to make about 15 crepes. Allow the crepes to fully cool.

Make the cream filling:

1. Beat the whipping cream with an electric mixer until stiff peaks form. Add the melted white chocolate and beat until the cream returns to stiff peaks.

2. Reserve ¼ of your filling and set aside. Place the remaining filling into 6 bowls, and dye these each a color of the rainbow. Keep your reserved filling white.

Assembly:

1. Place one crepe in the center of your desired serving dish. Arrange 5 crepes around the outer edges of the center crepe, slightly overlapping them and creating a flower-like shape. Spread some purple filling onto the center crepe and in between the overlapping edges, sealing the crepes together. Place another crepe in the center and spread the remaining purple filling evenly on top. Place another crepe on top and spread the blue filling over the surface.

continued on page 12

Repeat with another crepe and the green filling. Repeat until all of the crepes have been used and the filling is layered in the order of the rainbow.

2. Fold the 5 outer crepes on top of the cake and secure them with a ribbon wrapped around the perimeter of the cake. Fold the edges of the outer crepes back to look like a sack. Place the remaining white filling into a piping bag and pipe the filling onto the top of the sack.

3. Decorate with candy, yogurt pretzels, and Unicorn Poop Marshmallows. Place in the fridge and chill for 1–2 hours.

4. To serve, untie the ribbon and slice with a sharp knife. Enjoy!

TIP: *This cake can easily be personalized for any occasion! Dye the crepes or the filling any color you like and top with festive candies suited for your celebration.*

Unicorn Cake

This is a classic unicorn dessert and gets even better when sliced, revealing beautiful rainbow layers. Have fun decorating the unicorn's mane with sprinkles and any whimsical toppings you like!

Cake batter:

2 cups unsalted butter, room temperature
4 cups sugar
4 tsp. vanilla extract
12 eggs, room temperature
6 cups all-purpose flour
2 tsp. baking soda
2 tsp. salt
2½ cups sour cream
Pink, orange, yellow, green, blue, and purple food coloring

Buttercream:

3 cups unsalted butter, room temperature
1½ tsp. vanilla extract
7½ cups confectioner's sugar
Pink, yellow, green, blue, and black food coloring
2 tsp. vodka or clear peppermint extract
Edible glitter/shimmer dust
1 Edible Unicorn Horn (page 97)
1 jumbo marshmallow
Pink sanding sugar
Rainbow sprinkles

Bake the cake:

1. Place the butter and sugar in a bowl and beat with an electric mixer until pale and fluffy. Add the vanilla extract and eggs one at a time, mixing with each addition.

2. In a separate bowl, mix together the flour, baking soda, and salt. Add this to the butter mixture in 2 additions, alternating with sour cream.

3. Divide the batter between 6 bowls and dye them the colors of the rainbow. Pour each color into a greased and floured 8-inch round cake pan and bake at 350°F for 25–30 minutes, or until a skewer inserted into the cakes comes out clean.

4. Cool the cakes in the pans for 5 minutes, then transfer to a wire rack and cool completely.

5. Use a plate slightly smaller than the cakes as a guide to trim off the edges and create clean borders on all of the cakes.

Make the buttercream:

1. Beat the butter with an electric mixer until light and fluffy. Add the vanilla extract and beat until combined. Add the confectioner's sugar 1 cup at a time, then beat for 3–5 minutes until the buttercream is light and fluffy. Set aside.

Assembly:

1. Stack the cakes in the order of the rainbow. Spread about ⅓ cup of buttercream between each layer of cake.

2. Cover the entire surface of the cake in an even layer of buttercream.

continued on page 15

3. Divide 2 cups of the remaining buttercream between 4 bowls. Dye the buttercream pink, yellow, green, and blue. Dye 2 tbsp. of the remaining buttercream black. Place a piping bag fitted with a #2D star-shaped piping tip into a tall glass. Spread stripes of pink, yellow, green, and blue onto the insides of the piping bag, with each color taking up ¼ of the bag. Make sure to keep the center open. Dollop some white buttercream into the center of the piping bag, using a butter knife to gently coax it down into the center of the bag.

4. Pipe swirls onto the top of the cake, then pipe a mane down the back, curving towards the front of the cake. Pipe a large swirl onto the front of the cake, to create the unicorn's "bangs."

5. Dip a clean paintbrush into the vodka, then into the shimmer dust. Paint this onto the edible unicorn horn to create a golden sheen. Stick the unicorn horn onto the top of the cake. If it's too tall, use a serrated knife to gently cut off the base of the horn and shorten it.

6. To create the ears, cut a jumbo marshmallow in half diagonally with scissors. Stick the sticky sides of the marshmallow into pink sanding sugar, to create ears with pink centers. Stick the ears onto the top of the cake, on each side of the horn.

7. Place the black buttercream into a piping bag fitted with a #3 round piping tip. Pipe the eyes and eyelashes of the unicorn onto cake.

8. Decorate the unicorn's mane with rainbow sprinkles. Then slice to reveal the rainbow center and enjoy!

PEACH ROSE CHEESECAKE

This peach-flavored cheesecake is adorned with peach slices, arranged to look like a beautiful rose! While this may look intimidating, it's quite simple to do and will be the star of the show at your next potluck.

Cheesecake base:

5 tbsp. unsalted butter, melted

2⅓ cups graham crackers, crumbled into very small pieces

Cheesecake filling:

1¾ cups cream cheese, room temperature

6½ tbsp. sugar

1¾ cups whipping cream

¼ cup lemon juice

½ tsp. vanilla extract

5 tbsp. peach jam

2 tsp. powdered gelatin

2½ tbsp. water

Topping:

28-oz. can of peach halves (you'll need roughly 5–6 peach halves)

1 cup syrup from canned peaches

3 tsp. powdered gelatin

½ cup water

TIP: *Prefer a pink rose instead? Add a drop or two of pink food coloring to the jelly topping!*

1. First, make the base of the cheesecake. Combine the melted butter and crumbled graham crackers, then press them into the bottom of an 8-inch springform pan. Place this in the fridge while you make the filling.

2. To make the filling, place the cream cheese in a bowl and beat with an electric mixer until smooth. Add the sugar and combine. Then add the whipping cream, lemon juice, vanilla extract, and peach jam, and mix until smooth. Mix together the gelatin and water in a small bowl and microwave for 30 seconds. Add the gelatin to the filling, and mix together with an electric mixer until fully combined.

3. Pour the filling into the cake pan and return to the fridge to chill until set (approx. 3 hours).

4. Make the peach rose: Thinly slice the peach halves and arrange on the surface of the cake to make a rose pattern. Start from the outside of the cake and work inwards, slightly overlapping each peach slice to look like petals.

5. To make the jelly topping, pour the peach syrup into a small pot over medium heat. In a small bowl, combine the gelatin and ½ cup water, and mix together. Microwave for 30 seconds or until warm. Add to the pot, and mix well. Allow the mixture to cool for about 1–2 minutes, then gently pour the jelly over your layered peach slices.

6. Return the cheesecake to the fridge and chill until the jelly has set (approx 1½ hours). Carefully remove the cake from the springform pan by running a sharp knife around the edges of the cake, then release the sides of the pan and carefully slide off the cake. Enjoy!

Rainbow Unicorn Cupcakes

These adorable unicorn cupcakes have candles as their horns, making them a perfect treat for a birthday party!

Cake batter:

2 cups all-purpose flour
1 tsp. salt
3½ tsp. baking powder
½ cup unsalted butter, room temperature
1 cup sugar
1 tsp. vanilla extract
2 large eggs
1 cup milk
Pink, orange, yellow, green, blue, and purple food coloring

Buttercream:

2 cups unsalted butter, room temperature
1 tsp. vanilla extract
5 cups confectioner's sugar
Pink, yellow, green, blue, and black food coloring
24 mini marshmallows
Pink sanding sugar
White candles

Bake the cupcakes:

1. Combine the flour, salt, and baking powder in a bowl. In a separate bowl, cream the butter with an electric mixer until pale and fluffy. Add the sugar and mix. Add the vanilla and eggs and beat until combined. Add the dry ingredients in 2 additions, alternating with the milk. Divide the batter into 6 bowls and dye them each a color of the rainbow.

2. Dollop a small spoonful of each color of batter into each cup of a lined muffin tin (so each cupcake contains a dollop of each color). Bake the cupcakes at 350°F for 15–20 minutes, until fully cooked. Cool completely.

Make the buttercream:

1. Cream the butter with an electric mixer until pale and fluffy. Add the vanilla extract and combine. Add the confectioner's sugar one cup at a time, then beat for 3–5 minutes until fluffy.

To decorate:

1. Split your buttercream evenly, and leave one half white. Evenly coat the surface of the cupcakes with the white buttercream.

2. Divide the remaining buttercream into 6 bowls. Keep one bowl white and dye the remaining bowls pink, yellow, green, blue, and black. Place a piping bag fitted with a #20 star-shaped piping tip into a tall glass. Spread 4 stripes of white buttercream vertically onto the insides of the piping bag, evenly spacing them apart. Spread the pink buttercream into one open space and repeat with the yellow, green, and blue buttercream. Squeeze enough buttercream out of the tip until all 5 colors begin to come out. Place the black buttercream into a piping bag fitted with a #3 round piping tip.

3. Pipe swirls of buttercream to create the unicorns' mane, with a large dollop in the center where the horn will go.

4. Use scissors to cut the mini marshmallows in half diagonally, creating ears. Dip the cut, sticky side of the marshmallows into pink sugar to create the pinks of the ears. Stick the ears onto the cupcakes, then stick the candle horns into the cupcakes. Pipe the eyes and eyelashes onto the cupcakes with black buttercream and enjoy!

Mini Spiced Autumn Cheesecakes

Celebrate the beginning of fall with a cheesecake that reflects the changing colors of the leaves. This cheesecake is flavored with delicious fall spices, putting you in the mood for wool sweaters and apple cider!

Cheesecake base:

2⅓ cups graham crackers, crumbled into very small pieces
1 tsp. cinnamon
½ tsp. ground ginger
Pinch nutmeg
5 tbsp. unsalted butter, melted

Cheesecake filling:

1¾ cups cream cheese, room temperature
1 tsp. cinnamon
½ tsp. ground ginger
Pinch nutmeg
6 tbsp. sugar
1¾ cups whipping cream
¼ cup lemon juice
½ tsp. vanilla extract
5–6 tbsp. maple syrup
2 tsp. powdered gelatin
2½ tbsp. water

Leaf jellies:

2 cups water
6 tsp. sugar
1½ tsp. powdered agar
Red, orange, and yellow food coloring

Jelly topping:

1 cup water
2 tbsp. maple syrup
3 tsp. powdered gelatin
½ cup water

Make the cheesecake base:

1. Combine the graham crackers, cinnamon, ginger, and nutmeg. Add the butter and mix until fully combined. Divide this between four 4-inch springform pans and press down firmly with a spoon. Place in the fridge while you make the filling.

Make the cheesecake filling:

1. Place the cream cheese, cinnamon, ginger, and nutmeg in a bowl and beat with an electric mixer until smooth. Add the sugar and combine. Add the whipping cream, lemon juice, vanilla extract, and maple syrup and mix until smooth. In a separate bowl, combine the gelatin and water and microwave for 30 seconds. Add the gelatin to the filling and mix until fully combined.

2. Divide the filling between the pans and return to the fridge to chill until set, about 3 hours.

Make the leaf jellies:

1. Pour the water and sugar into a small pot and bring to a boil over medium heat. Add the powdered agar and simmer for 1 minute.

2. Divide the mixture into 2 plastic containers and allow to cool for 1 minute. Scatter droplets of red, orange, and yellow food coloring into the mixture and swirl with toothpicks until your desired pattern is reached. The jelly sets at room temperature, so make sure to work quickly.

continued on page 22

3. Once the jelly has fully set, slide the jelly out of the containers and use small cookie cutters to cut out flower or leaf shapes. Set the jellies aside.

Make the jelly topping:

1. Combine the water and maple syrup in a small pot and bring to a boil. While the water is heating up, combine the gelatin and ½ cup water. Microwave for 30 seconds. Add the gelatin to the pot and whisk until fully dissolved.

2. Pour into a glass with an easy-pour spout and cool to room temperature.

3. While the liquid is cooling, arrange the leaves on the surface of the cheesecakes. Gently pour the jelly topping on top and place the cheesecakes in the fridge until fully set.

4. To unmold the cheesecakes, run a sharp knife around the edge, then gently remove the sides of the pan. Enjoy!

Strawberry Cake

This fruity cake is packed with fresh strawberries and would be the perfect addition to a tea party!

Cake batter:

½ cup milk
2¼ tsp. white vinegar
2⅓ cups cake flour
1½ tsp. baking powder
½ tsp. baking soda
½ tsp. salt
1 tbsp. skim milk powder
(optional)
⅔ cup strawberry jam
1 tsp. vanilla extract
1 cup unsalted butter, softened
1¼ cups sugar
2 large eggs
4 large egg whites
Pink food coloring
1½ cups fresh strawberries,
finely chopped

Buttercream:

2 cups unsalted butter, room
temperature
1 tsp. vanilla extract
5 cups confectioner's sugar
1 tsp. matcha green tea powder
Pink food coloring
½ cup strawberry jam
¼ cup mini dark chocolate
chips

¼ cup dark chocolate chips

Bake the cake:

1. Mix together the milk and vinegar in a small bowl. Place this in the fridge for 15 minutes for the milk to slightly curdle. This is homemade buttermilk!

2. Sift all dry ingredients into a bowl and mix together. In a separate bowl, combine the jam, buttermilk, and vanilla extract. Set both bowls aside.

3. In a large bowl, whip the butter and sugar together with an electric mixer until pale and fluffy. Then add the eggs and egg whites one at a time, mixing after each addition. Add the flour mixture to the egg mixture in 3 additions, alternating with the buttermilk mixture, gently mixing after each addition. Then add the pink food coloring and diced strawberries and mix until just combined.

4. Pour the batter into one buttered 9-inch round cake pan. Bake at 350°F for 1 hour or until fully cooked. Transfer to a cooling rack and cool in the pan for about 10 minutes, then remove from the pan and place directly on the wire rack to cool completely.

Make the buttercream:

1. Cream the butter with an electric mixer until pale and fluffy. Add vanilla extract and beat until combined. Add confectioner's sugar one cup at a time, then beat for 3–5 minutes, until fluffy.

2. Place about ⅕ of the buttercream in a small bowl. Add the matcha green tea powder and mix well. Add a few drops of pink food coloring and the strawberry jam to the remaining vanilla buttercream and mix well.

continued on page 25

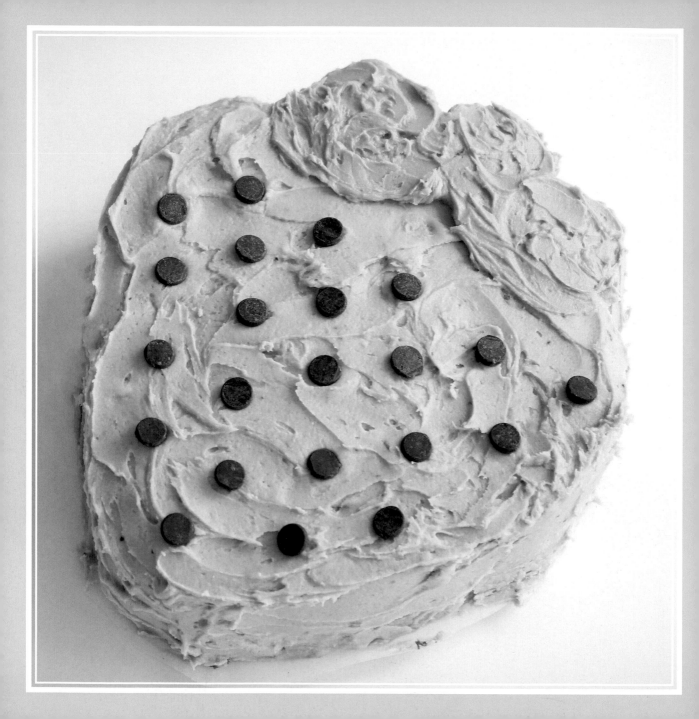

To assemble:

1. Once the cake has fully cooled, slice the cake in half to create two layers. Stack the layers on top of each other and slice them into a strawberry shape.

2. Place one cake on a serving platter of your choice, and place a large dollop of buttercream between the layers, spreading the buttercream about ½ inch from the edges of the cake. Sprinkle the mini chocolate chips on top of the buttercream to create "seeds" inside the cake. Top with the second layer of cake, then spread a thin layer of buttercream over the entire cake as a crumb coat. This will ensure that any crumbs don't get caught in the outer buttercream layer. Make sure to coat the "leaves" of the strawberries with the green matcha buttercream for the crumb coat. Place the cake in the fridge for about 20 minutes.

3. Coat the cake in a thick, fluffy layer of buttercream, coating the strawberry in pink and the leaves in green buttercream. Then stick the dark chocolate chips pointy side down onto the cake to look like seeds. Enjoy!

Rainbow Cake Pops

Bite into these delicious cake pops to reveal a colorful center inside!

For each cake pop color:

1 cup colored cake (see Unicorn Cake recipe
  on page 13)
⅓ cup white chocolate chips
2 tbsp. whipping cream

Coating, for all cake pops:

40 lollipop sticks
6 cups white chocolate chips, melted
Red, orange, yellow, green, blue, and purple
  sanding sugar

Make the cake pop filling:

1. Start with pink cake and repeat these steps with the orange, yellow, green, blue, and purple cake.

2. Slice any browning or crust off the cake, then break apart into fine crumbs.

3. In a pan, heat the white chocolate chips and whipping cream over low heat until the chocolate has melted and is combined with the cream.

4. Pour the chocolate and cream mixture into the cake crumbs, and mix everything together. Divide the mixture into 7 portions.

5. Shape each portion into a ball and place them on a tray lined with plastic wrap. Place the tray in the fridge for 15 minutes until they stiffen. Reshape the cake pops into balls and return to the fridge for 10 more minutes.

6. Repeat with the other colors of cake, to create pink, orange, yellow, green, blue, and purple cake pops—you will need to reheat another ⅓ cup chips and cream for each color.

7. Dip the tips of the lollipop sticks into the melted white chocolate one stick at a time, then stick them into the cakes. Return these to the fridge for 5 minutes, for the chocolate to set.

8. Dip each cake pop into the melted white chocolate, allowing the excess chocolate to drip into the bowls.

9. As soon as you dip them, sprinkle coordinating sanding sugar on top of each cake pop.

10. Return the cake pops to the tray and place in the fridge until the chocolate has fully set, about 20 minutes.

11. Enjoy!

Mousse Cakes

These vibrant mousse cakes are as light as air and taste of sweet vanilla and creamy white chocolate.

Cake base:

⅓ cup all-purpose flour
⅓ cup sugar
3 tbsp. cocoa powder
¼ tsp. baking powder
¼ tsp. baking soda
Pinch salt
½ large egg, beaten
2 tbsp. milk
1½ tbsp. oil
¼ tsp. vanilla extract
2 tbsp. water

Mousse:

3 tsp. gelatin
4½ tbsp. cold water
5 egg whites
¾ tsp. vanilla extract
1⅔ cups whipping cream
2¼ cups white chocolate
½ cup milk
Pink, orange, yellow, green, blue, and
   purple food coloring

Bake the cake base:

1. Place the flour, sugar, cocoa powder, baking powder, baking soda, and salt in the bowl of an electric mixer and mix on low speed until fully combined. Add the egg, milk, oil, vanilla, and water, and mix until smooth.

2. Line the sides and bottom of four 4-inch springform pans with parchment paper, and pour the batter into the pans. Bake at 350°F for 20–30 minutes, or until a skewer inserted into the center comes out clean. Place the pans on a cooling rack and cool completely. Remove the cakes from the pans and remove the parchment paper lining. If the cakes have risen, slice with a serrated knife to flatten the tops. Return the cakes to the pans and set aside.

Make the mousse layers:

1. Sprinkle the gelatin into the cold water and set aside. Beat the egg whites until stiff peaks form.

2. In a separate bowl, combine the whipping cream and vanilla extract and beat until soft peaks form. Set both bowls aside.

3. Set a small saucepan to medium heat and add the milk. Just before the milk comes to a boil, turn off the heat and add the gelatin. Once the gelatin has fully dissolved, add the white chocolate and whisk until fully melted. You may need to turn the heat back on to fully melt the chocolate.

4. Add this mixture to the whipped cream and whisk to combine. Then add the egg whites and whisk to combine, making sure to keep the mixture as airy as possible.

5. Divide the mixture into 6 bowls and dye them pink, orange, yellow, green, blue, and purple, folding each mixture gently to keep it light and airy.

6. Pour the purple mousse on top of the cakes and smooth the surface. Transfer the cakes to the freezer to set for 10 minutes. Gently pour the blue mousse on top, smooth the surface, and return the cakes to the freezer for 10 minutes. Repeat with the remaining colors, ending with pink.

7. Place the cakes in the fridge and chill for 2 hours.

8. Run a warm, damp dishcloth around the sides of the pans, then slide a sharp knife along the inside walls of the pans to help loosen the cakes. Gently unlatch the sides of the pans and slide off the cakes. Slice and enjoy!

Swiss Roll Cake

This cake is decorated within the cake batter! Spoon the cake batter into the pan any way you like to create your own unique pattern.

Cake:

4 large eggs
⅓ cup sugar
¼ cup water
8 tsp. vegetable oil
1 tsp. vanilla extract
⅔ cup cake flour
1 tsp. cornstarch
Pink, orange, yellow, green, and blue food coloring

Syrup:

3 tsp. sugar
4 tsp. hot water

Filling:

⅔ cup whipping cream
4 tsp. sugar
1 tsp. vanilla extract
½ cup chopped strawberries

Prep:

1. Place a sheet of parchment paper into a square 9x9-inch baking pan, and make little slices in the corners so that it fits snugly into the pan. Then lightly grease the parchment paper with a paper towel dipped in vegetable oil.

2. Divide the 4 eggs so that you have a bowl with 4 egg whites and a bowl with 3 egg yolks. You do not need the remaining 1 egg yolk.

Bake the cake:

1. Whisk together the 3 egg yolks in a bowl, and add half the sugar. Beat with a hand mixer until it lightens in color. Add the water, vegetable oil, and vanilla extract, and mix together.

2. Sift in the cake flour, and mix until the batter thickens and is a ribbon-like consistency. This will be called the Egg Yolk Batter.

3. Beat the 4 egg whites in a separate bowl with a hand mixer until they are glossy and reach stiff peaks. Then add the remaining sugar, and when the mixture develops a shine to it, add the cornstarch and mix again. This will be referred to as the Meringue.

5. Add the Meringue to the Egg Yolk Batter in 3 batches, and mix well until it is well-combined and has a ribbon-like consistency. Divide the mixture into 5 bowls and dye them pink, orange, yellow, green, and blue, folding very gently to keep the mixture airy.

continued on page 32

6. Drizzle each color of batter into the cake pan. Smooth out the surface, and tap it on the countertop a few times to remove the air. Bake at 340°F for 14 minutes.

7. Once it is finished baking, place a sheet of parchment paper on the surface of the cake, and flip it over onto a cooling rack.

8. Immediately peel off the parchment paper from the top of the cake and place another sheet of parchment paper on top. Allow the cake to cool completely, approximately 15 minutes.

Make the cream filling and syrup:

1. Place the cream and sugar in a bowl. Then place the bottom of the bowl in ice water, and whip until the cream stiffens. Add a few drops of vanilla extract.

2. Make the syrup: Dissolve the sugar in the hot water.

Assembly:

1. Once the cake has cooled, flip the cake over once more and peel off the parchment paper. Diagonally slice off just the corner ends of the cake; it will fit together nicely when rolled.

2. Using a serrated knife, make shallow slices ½" apart on the surface of the cake, being careful not to cut through the layer. Brush the syrup onto the cake with a pastry brush.

3. Spread the cream onto the cake, stopping about 1 inch from one end of the cake. Then place the strawberries on top.

4. Lift up the side of the cake and the parchment paper closest to you, and roll the cake away from you in one motion. Then continue to tightly roll the cake up with a firm grip. If the cake doesn't roll up very tightly, you can wrap the cake in plastic wrap to help. Twist the sides of the parchment paper closed like a candy wrapper, and place it in the fridge for 1 hour.

5. After the cake has rested, slice the ends of the cake off with a warm knife. This allows you to cleanly slice through the cake and cream.

6. Then serve and enjoy!

Naturally-Dyed Rainbow Cake

If you're not a fan of food coloring, this cake is perfect! The cake and the buttercream are naturally colored with juice and jam, which also moisten the cake and make this a dessert you definitely don't want to miss out on!

Cake batter:

2 cups unsalted butter, room temperature
4 cups sugar
4 tsp. vanilla extract
12 eggs, room temperature
6 cups all-purpose flour
2 tsp. baking soda
2 tsp. salt
2½ cups buttermilk
¼ cup canned beets
¼ cup canned carrots
¼ cup blueberries
¼ cup blackberries
1 tsp. turmeric
2 tsp. matcha green tea powder
8 tbsp. water

Buttercream:

3 cups unsalted butter, room temperature
1½ tsp. vanilla extract
7½ cups confectioner's sugar
2 tbsp. raspberry jam
1 tsp. turmeric
2 tbsp. peach jam
½ tsp. matcha green tea powder
2 tbsp. blueberry jam
2 tbsp. blackberry jam

Bake the cake:

1. Place the butter and sugar in a bowl and beat with an electric mixer until pale and fluffy. Add the vanilla extract and eggs one at a time, mixing with each addition.

2. In a separate bowl, mix together the flour, baking soda, and salt. Add this to the butter mixture in 2 additions, alternating with the buttermilk.

3. Divide the batter between 6 bowls.

4. Working with one ingredient at a time, pulse the canned beets, canned carrots, blueberries, and blackberries in a food processor, along with 2 tbsp. of water per ingredient. These will be used to dye the cake, so make sure to puree one ingredient with 2 tbsp. water at a time, rinsing the food processor between each ingredient.

5. Add the beet puree, carrot puree, turmeric, matcha green tea powder, blueberry puree, and blackberry puree each to a bowl of batter. The colors won't be as vibrant as when using food coloring, but they will still be beautiful!

6. Pour each color into a separate greased and floured 8-inch round cake pan and bake at 350°F for 25–30 minutes, or until a skewer inserted into the cakes comes out clean.

continued on page 35

7. Cool the cakes in the pans for 5 minutes, then transfer to a wire rack and cool completely.

8. Use a plate slightly smaller than the cakes as a guide to trim off the edges and create clean borders on all of the cakes.

Make the buttercream:

1. Beat the butter with an electric mixer until light and fluffy. Add the vanilla extract and beat until combined. Add the confectioner's sugar 1 cup at a time, then beat for 3–5 minutes until the buttercream is light and fluffy. Set aside.

Assembly:

1. Stack the cakes on a serving platter from darkest to lightest, spreading about ⅓ cup buttercream between each layer. Place the cake in the fridge for 10 minutes, then coat the entire surface of the cake in a thin layer of buttercream.

2. Divide the remaining buttercream into 6 bowls. Use the raspberry jam, turmeric, peach jam, matcha green tea powder, blueberry jam, and blackberry jam to dye the buttercream various colors. Place each color into piping bags fitted with #2A piping tips.

3. Working with the raspberry buttercream first, pipe dollops of buttercream in a vertical line down the side of the cake. Hold an offset spatula or a butter knife horizontally, then press into the center of each dollop and drag to the right. This will create a thumbprint-like effect. Repeat with the remaining dollops. Pipe a line of dollops with the turmeric buttercream on top of the "tails" of the raspberry buttercream, then repeat with the dragging technique and a clean knife. Repeat with the remaining colors of buttercream, returning to the raspberry buttercream once you've reached the end of the rainbow.

4. Once the entire cake has been decorated, repeat this technique on the top surface of the cake.

5. Then slice to reveal the naturally colored cake layers and enjoy!

Summer Beach Cake

Blue ombré cakes are stacked high and filled with vanilla buttercream, reminiscent of beautiful beach waves!

Cake:

1 cup unsalted butter, room temperature
2 cups sugar
1 tsp. vanilla extract
6 eggs, room temperature
3 cups all-purpose flour
1 tsp. baking soda
1 tsp. salt
1¼ cups sour cream
Blue food coloring

Buttercream:

1 cup unsalted butter, room temperature
½ tsp. vanilla extract
2½ cups confectioner's sugar
½ cup white meltable candy discs, melted
⅓ cup brown sugar

Bake the cake:

1. Beat the butter and sugar with an electric mixer until pale and fluffy. Add the vanilla extract and eggs one a time, mixing with each addition.

2. In a separate bowl, combine the flour, baking soda, and salt. Add this to the batter in 2 additions, alternating with the sour cream.

3. Divide the batter between 4 bowls. Keep one bowl white and dye the remaining bowls pale, medium, and dark blue, starting with just 1–2 drops for the pale. Pour the batter into 4 greased and floured 8-inch round cake pans. Bake at 350°F for 20 minutes, or until a skewer inserted into the cakes comes out clean.

Cool in the pans for 10 minutes, then transfer to a wire rack and cool completely.

Make the buttercream:

1. Beat the butter with an electric mixer until pale and fluffy. Add the vanilla extract and beat until combined. Add the confectioner's sugar one cup at a time, then beat for 3–5 minutes, until fluffy.

Assembly:

1. Using a plate as a guide, trim off the edges of all cakes. This will make them look pretty when they are being stacked. Also remove any excess browning from the tops and bottoms of the cakes.

2. Stack the cakes, starting with the dark blue cake and transitioning to the white cake, spreading a generous amount of buttercream between each layer. Spread the buttercream right to the edges of the cakes. Then spread a thin layer of buttercream on top of the cake.

3. Holding an offset spatula vertically against the surface of the cake, rotate the cake to smooth the buttercream filling between the layers.

4. Sprinkle some brown sugar on top of the cake to look like sand. Press some brown sugar into a shot glass, then turn out onto the top of the cake.

5. Pour some melted white candy melts into a seashell chocolate mold and place in the freezer until set, about 20 minutes. Unmold and decorate the cake.

6. Enjoy!

Other Baked Goodies

Rainbow-Filled Doughnuts

These doughnuts taste just like they're home from the bakery! Bite in to reveal the Rainbow Vanilla Pudding center.

2 tbsp. active dry yeast
½ cup warm water
¼ cup + 1 tsp. granulated sugar
2½ cups all-purpose flour
2 large eggs
2 tbsp. unsalted butter, room temperature
2 tsp. salt
Canola oil

Glaze:

1½ cups confectioner's sugar
½ cup whipping cream

Filling:

2½ cups Rainbow Vanilla Pudding
   (see page 93)
Pink, orange, yellow, green, blue, and purple
   food coloring
Rainbow sprinkles

Make the doughnuts:

1. Place the yeast, warm water, and 1 tsp. granulated sugar into the bowl of an electric mixer fitted with the dough hook attachment. Allow this to sit for 10 minutes, until the yeast begins to develop.

2. Add the flour, ¼ cup sugar, eggs, butter, and salt. Set the mixer to medium speed and knead for 8–9 minutes, until the dough is smooth, soft, and bounces back when poked with your finger.

3. Place the dough in an oiled bowl and cover with plastic wrap. Place in a warm spot until doubled in size, about 1 hour.

4. Roll the dough out to ¼ inch thick and cut into 2½-inch-wide circles with a cookie cutter. You should be able to get 15–20 doughnuts. Transfer the doughnuts to a lightly floured baking sheet and cover with a sheet of plastic wrap. Place in a warm spot and let rise for 20 minutes.

5. Pour about 5 inches of canola oil into a pot and set to medium heat. Attach a deep-fry thermometer and heat the oil to 370°F. Fry 3 or 4 doughnuts at a time, cooking for 1 minute on each side or until golden.

6. Remove the doughnuts from the oil with a slotted spoon and place on a baking sheet lined with paper towel. Cool completely.

Make the glaze:

1. Combine the confectioner's sugar and whipping cream in a bowl. Set aside.

Prep the filling:

1. Place all 6 colors of pudding into individual piping bags fitted with round piping tips.

Assembly:

1. Poke a hole in the side of each doughnut with the end of a fork. Pipe a dollop of each color of pudding into each doughnut in the order of the rainbow.

2. Dunk the doughnuts into the glaze, then sprinkle with rainbow sprinkles. Enjoy!

Unicorn Nest Pavlovas

Ever wondered where unicorns live? In soft, airy pavlovas, of course!

4 egg whites
1¼ cups sugar
2 tsp. vanilla extract, divided
1 tsp. fresh lemon juice
2 tsp. cornstarch
1 cup whipping cream
Yellow chocolate mini eggs
Gold shimmer dust
Rainbow candy belts
Mini marshmallows
Rainbow sprinkles
Edible gold glitter

TIP: *If making these in advance, the pavlova can be stored for 24 hours after baking and assembled right before serving.*

Make the meringues:

1. Beat the egg whites until stiff peaks form. Gradually add the sugar 1 tablespoon at a time, beating well with each addition. Once the mixture becomes glossy, fold in 1 tsp. vanilla extract, lemon juice, and cornstarch.

2. Drop dollops of the meringue onto 2 baking sheets lined with parchment paper, slightly building the edges of the dollops. Bake at 300°F for 25 minutes, until lightly browned and sound hollow when you tap them. Cool them for 10 minutes on the baking sheet, then transfer to a wire rack and cool completely.

Assembly:

1. Combine the whipping cream and 1 tsp. vanilla extract and beat until soft peaks form.

2. Dampen a clean paintbrush with water and dip into the gold shimmer dust. Paint the chocolate eggs to make them look golden!

3. To assemble, dollop some cream on top of the pavlovas and arrange the rainbow candy belts to look like a rainbow. Stick some mini marshmallows at the base to look like clouds. Place some golden eggs into the center and sprinkle rainbow sprinkles and gold glitter on top. Enjoy!

Unicorn Brick Toast

This is a shareable dessert, although it's definitely one you'll want to keep to yourself! The brick is filled with cubes of bread, caramelized with condensed milk, creating a deliciously sweet and sticky treat. Ice cream, unicorn horns, and sweets are piled high onto the loaf and taste delicious with the bread cubes!

1 loaf of unsliced white bread
¼ cup condensed milk
3 sliced strawberries + extra whole strawberries for topping
1 Edible Unicorn Horn (page 97)
2 scoops strawberry ice cream
2 white chocolate squares
2 strawberry wafer cookies
⅛ cup rainbow mini marshmallows
Sprinkles

1. First, make the bread bricks. Slice one end of the loaf of bread so that it's a square shape. Then cut out a cube of bread from the inside of the loaf, leaving about ½ inch from all four edges of the bread. Then pull the cube out, hollowing out your loaf, and cut into smaller, ¾-inch cubes. Place these on a baking sheet lined with parchment paper.

2. Brush the insides of the loaf with condensed milk. Brush condensed milk onto the small bread cubes, leaving one side bare. Bake at 375°F for 10 minutes.

3. Fill the loaf with the bread cubes and the sliced strawberries, and then top with 2 scoops of ice cream and an Edible Unicorn Horn. Top with some fresh strawberries, chocolate squares, and strawberry wafer cookies, and then sprinkle some mini marshmallows and sprinkles on top.

4. To eat, slice open the loaf and dip the delicious, caramelized bread cubes into the ice cream scoops.

SPIRAL COOKIES

These sugar cookies are made just like a jelly roll cake—just roll and slice away!

½ cup granulated sugar
2 tbsp. confectioner's sugar
¼ tsp. salt
1 large egg
1 tsp. vanilla extract
1 cup unsalted butter, room temperature
2 cups all-purpose flour
Pink, orange, yellow, green, blue,
 and purple food coloring

1. Combine the granulated sugar, confectioner's sugar, and salt in a bowl. In a separate bowl, combine the egg and vanilla extract. Set both bowls aside.

2. Beat the butter with an electric mixer until pale and fluffy. Add the sugar mixture and mix until combined. Add the egg mixture and combine. Gradually add the flour and mix until just combined.

3. Divide the dough into 2 balls and set one ball aside. Divide the other ball into 6 pieces and dye each piece a color of the rainbow.

4. Sandwich the uncolored dough between 2 sheets of floured parchment paper and roll out into a 10x12-inch rectangle. Roll each colored ball of dough into a long sausage shape and line them up on another sheet of floured parchment paper. Make sure to line them up so that the long edges only show one color of dough and the short edges show all 6 – this will create the rainbow pattern when rolling the dough later. Gently press together and place another sheet of floured parchment paper on top. Roll out into a 10x12-inch rectangle. Stack the sheets on a baking sheet and place in the fridge for 1 hour.

5. Remove the top sheet of parchment paper from both sheets of dough and flip the rainbow dough on top of the uncolored dough. Trim the edges. Position the dough with the long edge facing you and roll the dough away into a spiral, like a jelly roll. Roll the dough tightly in plastic wrap and place in the freezer for 1 hour.

6. Slice the dough into ¼ inch thick slices and place on a baking sheet lined with parchment paper. Bake at 325°F for 14 minutes, until the edges are just slightly golden. Cool completely and enjoy!

Rainbow Baked Doughnuts

These doughnuts are so soft and fluffy and are a fantastic alternative to fried doughnuts. They can be whipped up in under an hour, making them perfect for afternoon snacking!

Doughnut batter:

1 cup all-purpose flour
1 tsp. baking powder
¼ tsp. salt
3 tbsp. unsalted butter, melted
¼ cup sugar
2 tbsp. honey
1 large egg
½ tsp. vanilla extract
⅓ cup + 1 tbsp. buttermilk
Pink, orange, yellow, green, blue, and purple food coloring

Glaze:

3 tbsp. whipping cream
1 cup confectioner's sugar
Rainbow sprinkles

Bake the doughnuts:

1. Whisk together the flour, baking powder, and salt in a small bowl and set aside. In a large bowl, combine the butter, sugar, honey, egg, and vanilla extract. Add the buttermilk and mix until combined. Add the dry ingredients and milk until just combined—make sure not to overmix. Divide the mixture into 6 bowls and dye them the colors of the rainbow.

2. Spoon one color of batter at a time into a greased doughnut pan, creating a rainbow pattern. Bake at 400°F for 7 minutes. Cool for 1 minute in the pan, then flip the pan over to remove the doughnuts and cool completely on a wire rack.

Make the glaze:

1. Whisk together the whipping cream and the confectioner's sugar and whisk until fully combined.

2. Dunk each doughnut into the glaze and return to the wire rack. Top with rainbow sprinkles and enjoy!

Rainbow Confetti Cookies

Bite into these cookies and rainbow sprinkles come pouring out!

Cookie dough:

2 cups flour
¼ tsp. salt
½ tsp. baking powder
Pinch ground cinnamon
¼ cup confetti sprinkles
½ cup unsalted butter
1 cup sugar
2 tbsp. milk
1 large egg
½ tsp. vanilla extract

Royal icing:

½ lb. confectioner's sugar
2½ tbsp. meringue powder
Scant ¼ cup water
Pink, yellow, green, blue and purple
    food coloring
½ cup rainbow sprinkles

Bake the cookies:

1. Mix together the flour, salt, baking powder, cinnamon, and confetti sprinkles in a bowl. In a separate bowl, cream the butter and sugar with an electric mixer until it becomes light and fluffy. Add the milk, egg, and vanilla, and mix well. Then slowly add the flour mixture until it is just combined.

2. Shape the dough into a ball, then divide it in half. Wrap each in plastic wrap and place in the refrigerator for 1 hour.

3. Roll the cookie dough out until ¼-inch thick and cut into circle shapes with a 4-inch round cookie cutter. Then slice each circle in half, creating 2 half circles. For 1 cookie, you will need 3 half circles.

4. Transfer to a baking sheet lined with parchment paper. Cut out the centers of ⅓ of the cookies.

5. Bake the cookies at 350°F for 10 minutes, or until the edges are just starting to brown. Transfer to a wire rack and cool completely.

Make the royal icing:

1. Combine the confectioner's sugar and meringue powder in a large bowl. Add the water and beat for 7 minutes, until it is smooth and when drizzled stays on the surface for a few seconds.

2. Divide the icing into 5 bowls and dye them pink, yellow, green, blue, and purple. Place each color into piping bags fitted with #3 round piping tips.

Assembly:

1. Pipe a border of any color of icing around the edges of half of the whole cookies and place the cookies missing their centers on top.

2. Spoon the sprinkles into the center, making sure not to add so many sprinkles that they rise past the top of the cookie.

3. Pipe some more icing around the borders of the top cookie, then place another whole cookie on top. Gently press down to seal closed.

4. Pipe thick rainbow stripes onto the cookies, creating pastel rainbows. Allow the icing to dry completely, about 1 hour.

5. Then bite into the cookies and watch as the sprinkles fall out!

TIP: *This is a fun technique that can be used as gender-reveal cookies for a baby shower, using pink or blue sprinkles!*

Rainbow Ombré Shortbread

This shortbread is so buttery, it melts in your mouth. It's impossible to stop at just one cookie!

½ cup unsalted butter, room temperature
¼ cup confectioner's sugar
1 tsp. vanilla extract
1 cup all-purpose flour
Heaping ¼ tsp. salt
Pink, orange, yellow, green, blue, and purple
   food coloring

1. Beat the butter with an electric mixer until light and fluffy. Add the confectioner's sugar and beat until fluffy. Add the vanilla extract and beat until combined. In a separate bowl, combine the flour and salt, then add to the butter mixture, mixing until the dough sticks together when pinched with fingers.

2. Divide the dough into 6 balls and dye them the colors of the rainbow. Roll the balls out into long sausage shapes and line them up on a sheet of plastic wrap. Cover with another sheet of plastic wrap. Press them together with a rolling pin to create an ombré effect and seal the colors together. Transfer the dough to the freezer for 15 minutes, or until firm.

3. Use your desired cookie cutter to cut out shapes and arrange on a baking sheet lined with parchment paper. Refrigerate for 30 minutes, then bake at 325°F for 10–15 minutes, or until the edges are just slightly golden. Cool on the baking sheet for 10 minutes, then transfer to a wire rack and cool completely.

RAINBOW MACARONS

Macarons may seem intimidating, but they're actually quite easy! Just follow the directions step-by-step and you'll have beautiful macarons every single time.

1 cup confectioner's sugar
¾ cup almond flour (not almond meal)
2 large egg whites
Pinch cream of tartar
¼ cup superfine sugar
1 tsp. vanilla extract
Red, orange, yellow, green, and blue food coloring
Raspberry jam, or any filling of your choice

1. Combine first two ingredients, and sift 3 times.

2. Place egg whites in a large bowl and beat with an electric mixer until foamy. Add the cream of tartar, then beat until soft peaks form. Add sugar and beat on high speed until stiff peaks form. Add the vanilla extract and gently mix to combine. Sift the dry mixture into the egg mixture and gently fold to combine.

3. Place ¼ of the batter into a piping bag fitted with a #2A round piping tip. Divide remaining batter into 5 bowls and dye them red, orange, yellow, green, and blue. Place the batter into piping bags fitted with #8 round piping tips.

4. Prepare a baking sheet lined with parchment paper or a Silpat mat. To create the rainbows, pipe large arches with the red batter. Pipe arches with the remaining colors, working in the order of the rainbow. To create the clouds, position the piping bag with the white batter straight downwards and pipe 4–5 dollops onto the baking sheet.

5. Tap the baking sheets on your countertop a couple times to remove any air bubbles. Let the macarons sit at room temperature for 30 minutes.

6. Set your oven to 375°F, heat for 5 minutes, then reduce the heat to 325°F. Bake the macarons, one sheet at a time, for 6–8 minutes, rotating halfway through. After each batch, increase the heat to 375°F, heat for 5 minutes, then reduce to 325°F and pop the next sheet into the oven.

7. Allow the macarons to cool on the sheet for 2–3 minutes, then transfer to a wire rack and cool completely.

8. Sandwich some raspberry jam between the macarons and enjoy!

Candy Cane Doughnuts

These red and white swirled doughnuts taste like festive candy canes! Serve these with candy cane ice cream or Peppermint Frozen Hot Chocolate (page 115).

Doughnut batter:

1 cup all-purpose flour
1 tsp. baking powder
¼ tsp. salt
3 tbsp. unsalted butter, melted
¼ cup sugar
2 tbsp. honey
1 large egg
¼ tsp. vanilla extract
1 tsp. peppermint extract
⅓ cup + 1 tbsp. buttermilk
Red food coloring

Glaze:

3 tbsp. whipping cream
½ cup confectioner's sugar
5 crushed candy canes, for decorating

Bake the doughnuts:

1. Whisk together the flour, baking powder, and salt in a small bowl and set aside. In a large bowl, combine the butter, sugar, honey, egg, vanilla, and peppermint extract. Add the buttermilk and mix until combined. Add the dry ingredients and mix until just combined—make sure not to overmix. Divide the mixture into 2 bowls and dye one bowl red.

2. Spoon the batter into a piping bag, placing the piping bag on its side and filling one side with one color, then spoon the other color on top. This will create a striped pattern when you pipe the batter into the pan! Pipe the batter into a greased doughnut pan and bake at 400°F for 7 minutes. Cool for 1 minute in the pan, then flip the pan over to remove the doughnuts and cool completely on a wire rack.

Make the glaze:

1. Whisk together the whipping cream and the confectioner's sugar until fully combined.

2. Dunk each doughnut into the glaze and return to the wire rack. Top with crushed candy canes and enjoy!

Lollipop Cookie Pops

These are such a fun, playful twist on traditional sugar cookies! They are deliciously chewy and perfect for popping into lunchboxes!

2 cups all-purpose flour
¼ tsp. salt
½ tsp. baking powder
½ cup unsalted butter, room temperature
1 cup sugar
2 tbsp. milk
1 large egg, beaten
1 tsp. vanilla extract
Pink, orange, yellow, green, blue, and purple food coloring
6 cookie pop sticks (these are thicker than regular lollipop sticks)

To make the cookies:

1. Mix together the flour, salt, and baking powder in a bowl. In a separate bowl, cream the butter and sugar with an electric mixer until it becomes light and fluffy. Add the milk, egg, and vanilla, and mix well. Then slowly add the flour mixture until it is just combined.

2. Shape the dough into a ball, then divide it into 6 balls. Dye them each a color of the rainbow, then divide each ball in half. Roll each ball into a 17-inch-long sausage-shape. You should have 2 sausages of each color. On a large sheet of plastic wrap, line up 1 of each color of sausage in the order of the rainbow, pressing them together. Wrap the edges of the plastic wrap around the dough and gently roll to seal all colors together.

3. Divide the sausage into 3 pieces, then twist each sausage to create a rainbow swirl. Repeat with the remaining sausages from Step 2, to create a total of 6 rainbow sausages.

4. Roll each sausage into a tight spiral shape. Prepare a baking sheet lined with parchment paper. Place the cookies onto the baking sheet, positioning a cookie pop stick halfway underneath.

5. Place the entire baking sheet in the freezer for 10 minutes, to firm the dough. Then bake at 350°F for 15 minutes, until the dough has ever so slightly browned at the edges.

6. Cool completely on the baking sheet and enjoy!

Confetti Fun Churros

These churros are so light and airy and highly addictive! They're coated in whimsical confetti sugar and are the perfect treat for date nights at home!

Topping:

⅓ cup confetti sprinkles
1 cup confectioner's sugar

Dipping sauce:

¼ cup dark chocolate, melted
2 tbsp. whipping cream, heated until hot
Pinch salt

Dough:

1 cup water
½ cup unsalted butter, cold and cut into cubes
2 tbsp. granulated sugar
¼ tsp. salt
1 cup all-purpose flour
½ cup confetti sprinkles
3 large eggs
5–6 cups vegetable oil, for frying

Make the topping:

1. Place the confetti sprinkles in a food processor and pulse until the sprinkles resemble a fine crumb. Combine with the confectioner's sugar and set aside.

Make the dipping sauce:

1. Combine the melted chocolate, whipping cream, and salt. Pour into a small dish and set aside.

Make the churros:

1. Place the water, butter, granulated sugar, and salt in a pot and set to medium-high heat. Bring to a boil, then reduce to low heat. Add the flour and ½ cup confetti sprinkles and mix until combined, for about 1 minute.

2. Place the dough in a large bowl and add the eggs one at a time, beating with an electric mixer.

3. Place the dough in a piping bag fitted with a #6B open star-shaped piping tip.

4. Pour the oil into a medium-sized pot and attach a deep-fry thermometer. Set to medium-high heat and heat to 325°F. Hover the piping bag a couple inches above the oil and pipe out 4–5-inch long churros, using scissors to snip them from the piping bag. Fry for 4 minutes per side, until golden brown.

5. Remove the churros from the oil with a slotted spoon and transfer to a plate lined with paper towel. Drain the excess oil.

6. Immediately roll the churros in the topping mixture and serve with the dipping sauce. Enjoy!

Pink Sparkly Doughnuts

The ultimate glamorous dessert! These vanilla doughnuts are dunked in edible glitter and are so beautiful and sparkly.

Doughnut batter:

1 cup all-purpose flour
1 tsp. baking powder
¼ tsp. salt
3 tbsp. unsalted butter, melted
¼ cup sugar
2 tbsp. honey
1 large egg
½ tsp. vanilla extract
⅓ cup + 1 tbsp. buttermilk
Pink food coloring

Glaze:

4 tbsp. whipping cream
1 cup confectioner's sugar
Pink food coloring
½ cup pink edible glitter

1. Whisk together the flour, baking powder, and salt in a small bowl and set aside. In a large bowl, combine the butter, sugar, honey, egg, and vanilla extract. Add the buttermilk and mix until combined. Add the dry ingredients and milk until just combined—make sure not to overmix. Dye the batter your desired shade of pink.

2. Spoon the batter into a greased doughnut pan. Bake at 400°F for 7 minutes. Cool for 1 minute in the pan, then flip the pan over to remove the doughnuts and cool completely on a wire rack.

3. Make the glaze: Whisk together the whipping cream and the confectioner's sugar and whisk until fully combined. Dye your desired shade of pink. Dunk each doughnut into the glaze and return to the wire rack. Dunk the glazed doughnuts directly into some pink edible glitter and enjoy!

Confetti Cream Puffs

These cream puffs are light and crisp and filled with a smooth vanilla pastry cream. For an extra luxurious touch, dip them in melted chocolate!

Dough:

1 cup water
½ cup unsalted butter, cold and cut into cubes
1 tsp. sugar
½ tsp. salt
1 cup all-purpose flour
4 large eggs
½ cup confetti sprinkles

Pastry cream:

½ cup sugar
¼ cup cornstarch
Pinch salt
2 cups milk
4 large egg yolks
2 tbsp. unsalted butter, cold
1½ tsp. vanilla extract
1 cup rainbow sprinkles

Make the cream puffs:

1. In a large pot, combine the water, butter, sugar, and salt. Set to high heat and bring to a boil. Stir in the flour with a wooden spoon mix until a film forms on the bottom of the pan. Transfer the dough to a bowl and cool for 3–4 minutes. Add the eggs one at a time, stirring vigorously and completely incorporating each egg after each addition. Add the confetti sprinkles and mix until combined.

2. Transfer the dough to a piping bag fitted with a #1A round piping tip and pipe 1½-inch rounds onto baking sheets lined with parchment paper. Wet your fingers and smooth any pointed peaks.

3. Bake them at 375°F for 30 minutes. Cool on the pan for 10 minutes, then transfer to a wire rack and cool completely.

Make the pastry cream:

1. Combine the sugar, cornstarch, and salt in a pot. Add the milk, egg yolks, and butter, and whisk together. Set to medium heat and whisk constantly until it comes to a boil. Once it thickens, remove from the heat and add the vanilla extract.

2. Strain through a sieve and cover with plastic wrap, pressing it directly on the surface. Refrigerate until chilled. If the pastry cream becomes lumpy, pulse in a food processor a couple times. Transfer to a piping bag fitted with a #2A round tip.

Assembly:

1. Slice the cream puffs in half. Pipe a generous dollop of cream between the two layers.

2. Sprinkle rainbow sprinkles onto the sides of the pastry cream and enjoy your cream puffs!

Mini Unicorn Pies

These pies are stuffed with a delicious cherry berry filling and are the perfect size to pop into lunchboxes or take on a picnic!

Pie crust:

5 cups all-purpose flour (plus extra for dusting)
2 tsp. salt
2 tsp. sugar
2 cups cold unsalted butter, cut into cubes
½ cup to 1 cup very cold water
Pink, orange, yellow, green, blue, and purple food coloring

Filling:

1 lb. frozen cherries, thawed
1 pint raspberries
1 pint blackberries
½ cup granulated sugar
2½ tbsp. cornstarch
2 tbsp. lemon juice

Make the pie crust:

1. Mix together the flour, salt, and sugar in a food processor. Add butter and pulse until it turns into a crumbly meal-like texture. Add the cold water and pulse until the dough sticks together when squished together.

2. Turn the dough out onto a floured surface and shape into a ball. Divide the dough into 6 balls and dye them pink, orange, yellow, green, blue, and purple. Divide each ball in half, then make 2 large balls of dough, each consisting of one ball of each color. Roughly shape each into a disk with your hands, then wrap in plastic wrap. Place these in the refrigerator for 1 hour until firm.

Make the filling:

1. In a large bowl, mix together the cherries, raspberries, blackberries, sugar, cornstarch, and lemon juice.

Assemble and bake:

1. Roll the dough out on a floured surface until it is ⅛-inch thick. Using a 4½-inch round cookie cutter, cut 12 circles out of the dough and press them into the bottom and sides of a muffin tin. Fill the cups with the pie filling.

2. Using a 3½-inch round cookie cutter, cut out 12 more circles and press them on top of each pie, sealing the bottom and top layers of dough tightly with your fingers. Slice an "x" in the center of each pie.

3. Bake at 400°F for 30 minutes. Cool in the pan for 10 minutes, then transfer to a cooling rack and enjoy!

CANDY

RAINBOW SUGAR CUBES

Sweeten up your morning coffee or tea with rainbows!

4 tsp. water
2 cups granulated sugar
Red, yellow, orange, green, blue, and purple
   food coloring

TIP: *These are perfect as a hostess gift or party favor! Simply package them in a cellophane bag and tie with a colorful ribbon.*

1. Combine the water and granulated sugar, mixing until it feels like damp sand. Divide into 6 bowls and dye each bowl of sugar a different color of the rainbow.

2. Using a small spoon, press the sugar into any mold of your choice, pressing down very firmly. Layer the sugar in the order of the rainbow. Once the molds are full, press down even more firmly with the side of a butter knife. Let sit at room temperature to dry out overnight.

3. Remove the sugar cubes from the mold, and enjoy!

Neapolitan Marshmallows

Add a delicious chocolate, vanilla, and strawberry touch to your hot chocolate with these soft, pillowy marshmallows! And once you try this homemade version, you'll never go back to store-bought!

Chocolate marshmallow:

2½ tsp. powdered gelatin
⅓ cup + ¼ cup cold water
1 cup sugar
1 tbsp cocoa powder
Cooking spray

Vanilla marshmallow:

2½ tsp. powdered gelatin
⅓ cup + ¼ cup cold water
1 cup sugar
Seeds from 1 vanilla bean

Strawberry marshmallow:

2½ tsp. powdered gelatin
⅓ cup + ¼ cup cold water
1 cup sugar
1 tsp. strawberry extract
Pink food coloring

½ cup confectioner's sugar
½ cup cornstarch

Make the chocolate layer:

1. Pour ⅓ cup of cold water into the bowl of an electric mixer and sprinkle the powdered gelatin on top. Let sit for 5 minutes.

2. Place the sugar and ¼ cup cold water in a small pot and set to medium-high heat. Stir until the sugar has melted.

3. Attach a candy thermometer to the pot and boil the sugar until it reaches 240°F. Brush the sides of the pot with a wet pastry brush if sugar crystals stick to the sides.

4. Add the hot sugar to the gelatin and stir the mixture by hand, whisking for a few minutes to slightly cool. Then beat with an electric mixer on medium-high speed for 8–10 minutes, until soft peaks form. Add the cocoa powder and mix until fully combined.

5. Line a jelly roll pan with parchment paper and generously coat with cooking spray.

6. Pour the chocolate marshmallow into the pan and spread to all corners of the pan, smoothing the surface. Set aside.

Make the vanilla layer:

1. Repeat steps 1–5, adding your vanilla bean seeds instead of cocoa powder.

2. Pour on top of the chocolate layer and smooth the surface. Set aside.

continued on page 74

Make the strawberry layer:

1. Repeat steps 1–5 with your strawberry flavor. Add a few drops of pink food coloring and mix well.

2. Pour on top of the vanilla layer and smooth the surface.

To finish:

1. Allow the marshmallow to sit at room temperature for 3–4 hours (or up to overnight) to stiffen.

2. In a small bowl, combine the confectioner's sugar and cornstarch. Place in a mesh sieve and dust over the entire surface of the marshmallow.

3. Cut the marshmallow into squares, then gently remove from the pan with the help of a butter knife or spatula. Dust more cornstarch mixture onto the freshly sliced, sticky edges of the marshmallows.

4. Place the marshmallows into the sieve and bounce them several times to remove any excess cornstarch mixture.

5. Eat these marshmallows as is, or enjoy with a cup of hot chocolate. These marshmallows are best served the same day, but can be stored for 1–2 days in a plastic container lined with parchment paper.

TIP: *While the base of each marshmallow layer is the same, it is important that you make them separately, instead of in one large batch. The marshmallow sets quite quickly, so making the layers one by one will create smooth layers and allow you to more evenly distribute the flavorings in each layer.*

Marshmallow Macarons

Macarons are adorable, but they're not limited to cookies! These raspberry vanilla marshmallows are quite at home in your hot chocolate and are a fun twist on classic marshmallows.

⅓ cup cold water
2½ tsp. powdered gelatin
1 cup sugar
¼ cup cold water
1 tsp. vanilla extract
2½ tsp. powdered gelatin
⅓ cup cold water
1 cup sugar
¼ cup cold water
Pink food coloring
½ tsp. raspberry (or strawberry) flavoring

1. Draw 2-inch circles onto a sheet of parchment paper, then flip the paper over and place onto a baking sheet. These circles will help guide you when piping the macarons.

2. Pour ⅓ cup of cold water into the bowl of an electric mixer and sprinkle the powdered gelatin on top. Let sit for 5 minutes.

3. Place the sugar and ¼ cup cold water in a small pot and set to medium-high heat. Stir until the sugar has melted.

4. Attach a candy thermometer to the pot and boil the sugar until it reaches 238°F. Brush the sides of the pot with a wet pastry brush if sugar crystals stick to the sides. Remove the pot from the heat and stir until the sugar stops boiling. Add the vanilla extract and stir to combine.

5. Add the hot sugar to the gelatin and stir the mixture by hand, whisking for a few minutes to slightly cool. Then beat with an electric mixer on medium-high speed for 8–10 minutes, until soft peaks form. Add a few drops of pink food coloring and mix until combined.

6. Place the marshmallow in a piping bag fitted with a #1A round piping tip. Point the tip downwards into the center of one circle on the prepared sheet of parchment paper, and squeeze until the marshmallow

continued on page 77

fills the circle, keeping the tip of the piping bag in one place. This will achieve an even, domed-shape macaron. Continue with the remaining marshmallow mixture.

7. Allow the marshmallows to sit at room temperature overnight to stiffen.

8. To make the filling, repeat steps 1–4, adding raspberry flavoring instead of vanilla extract and dyeing the marshmallow mixture a deeper shade of pink.

9. Peel the macarons off of the parchment paper and place them flat side up. Place the raspberry marshmallow into a piping bag fitted with a round tip and pipe some marshmallow onto half of the macarons. Place the empty halves on top to make macarons.

10. Allow the macarons to sit for 1–2 hours for the filling to dry to the touch, then enjoy! (Note: if you find that the marshmallows are too sticky, dust them in a combination of ¼ cup cornstarch and ¼ cup confectioner's sugar.)

Rainbow Hard Candies

Follow this simple technique to make homemade hard candy or lollipops in any flavor and color you desire!

2½ cups granulated sugar
1 cup water
1½ cups light corn syrup
Your desired flavoring and food coloring

TIP: *If using plastic lollipop molds, be sure to coat them generously in cooking spray before using.*

1. Place a pot over medium heat and add the granulated sugar, water, and light corn syrup. Stir with a rubber spatula until everything is melted and combined.

2. Increase to high heat and attach a candy thermometer to the pot. Stir the mixture occasionally. When it reaches 300°F, add the food coloring and mix well. Heat the sugar until it reaches 310°F, then remove from the heat and stir until it stops bubbling. Add the flavoring and mix until well-combined.

3. Pour into a silicone mold of your choice, and allow to fully harden at room temperature (about 30 minutes). Remove them from the mold, and enjoy!

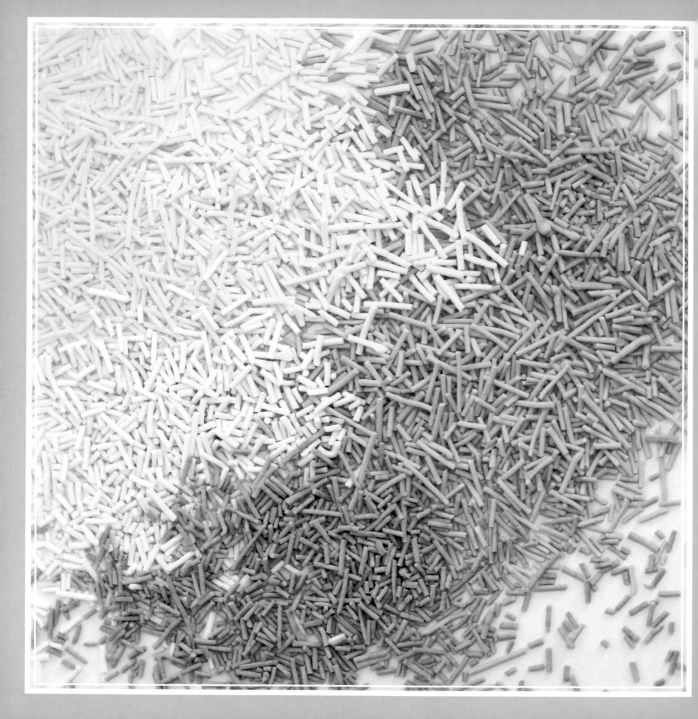

DIY Rainbow Sprinkles

This is the ultimate trick in personalizing desserts! Create neon, pastel, or vibrant rainbow sprinkles, or some to match the exact color scheme of your party.

1¾ cups confectioner's sugar
½ tsp. salt
1 egg white
1 tsp. vanilla extract, or your desired flavoring
Pink, orange, yellow, green, blue, and purple food coloring

1. Beat the confectioner's sugar, salt, egg white, and vanilla extract in a bowl with an electric mixer until it resembles a semi-thick paste.

2. Divide the paste into 6 bowls and dye each bowl a color of the rainbow.

3. Place the paste into piping bags fitted with #134 or #89 piping tips. Alternatively, any small, round piping tip will work.

4. Pipe long, thin lines onto a baking sheet lined with parchment paper. Make sure that the lines do not touch.

5. Allow the sprinkles to dry for a full 24 hours. Scrape the sprinkles off the sheet with a knife, then chop into pieces.

6. Store in an airtight container and enjoy!

Unicorn Poop Marshmallows

These playful marshmallows look so amusing atop hot chocolate! For a fun party favor, package each dollop in a cellophane bag and tie with a rainbow ribbon.

Marshmallows:

⅓ cup + ¼ cup cold water
2½ tsp. powdered gelatin
1 cup granulated sugar
½ vanilla bean pod (seeds only)
Pink, orange, yellow, green, blue, and purple
    food coloring

Sugar coating:

¼ cup confectioner's sugar
2 tbsp. cornstarch

1. Pour ⅓ cup of cold water into the bowl of an electric mixer and sprinkle the powdered gelatin on top. Let sit for 5 minutes.

2. Place the sugar and ¼ cup cold water in a small pot and set to medium-high heat. Stir until the sugar has melted. Attach a candy thermometer to the pot and boil the sugar until it reaches 238°F. Brush the sides of the pot with a wet pastry brush if sugar crystals stick to the sides.

3. Add the hot sugar to the gelatin and stir the mixture by hand, whisking for a few minutes to slightly cool. Beat with an electric mixer on medium-high speed for 8–10 minutes, until soft peaks form. Then add the vanilla bean seeds and mix well.

4. Divide the marshmallow into 6 bowls and dye them the colors of the rainbow. Place them into separate piping bags and snip about ½ inch off the ends of the bags with scissors. Hold the piping bags together and insert them all into another piping bag. Snip off the end of the bag, so that when gently squeezed, all of the colors flow out evenly from the tip. Work quickly at this stage—the marshmallow sets quickly at room temperature.

5. Pipe swirly dollops onto a baking sheet lined with parchment paper.

6. Allow the marshmallows to dry at room temperature for 5 hours.

7. In a small bowl, combine the confectioner's sugar and cornstarch. Place in a sieve and dust over the marshmallows. Use a butter knife or an offset spatula to gently peel the marshmallows off the parchment paper. Dust the bottoms of the marshmallows in the sugar coating.

8. Place the marshmallows in an empty sieve and bounce a couple times to remove any excess sugar coating.

9. Store in an airtight container for 1–2 days. Enjoy!

RAINBOW STRIPED JELLIES

To turn these into jelly shots, you can replace the 2 cups milk with flavored vodka!

Cooking spray
1½ cups + ¼ cup water
6 tbsp. gelatin
1 cup sweetened condensed milk
2 cups milk
1 tsp. vanilla extract
Pink, orange, yellow, green, blue, and purple
   food coloring
Whipped cream
Rainbow confetti sprinkles

1. Spray a 9x9-inch pan with cooking spray. Set aside.

2. Pour 1½ cups water into a pot and sprinkle the gelatin on top. Allow the gelatin to develop for 5 minutes. Set the pot to medium heat and whisk constantly until the gelatin has dissolved and is liquid. Remove the pot from the heat and add the condensed milk, whisking to combine. Add the milk, vanilla extract, and ¾ cup water and whisk until fully combined.

3. Divide the mixture between 6 microwave-safe bowls. Dye each a color of the rainbow.

4. Pour the pink layer into the pan and place in the fridge until set to the touch, about 20–30 minutes. Repeat with the other colors, working in the order of the rainbow. If the different colors of jelly begin to set before you pour them into the dish, microwave them for 10-second intervals, until liquid again. Then chill in the refrigerator for 6 hours or up to overnight.

5. Gently pull the sides of the jelly away from the pan with your fingers. Place a plate on top and flip the pan upside down, unmolding the jelly. Use a sharp knife to slice the jelly into squares. Top with some whipped cream and sprinkles and enjoy!

Candy Heart Coconut Dumplings

These dumplings are wonderfully chewy and coated in a delicious coconut ginger syrup.

Dumplings:

⅔ cup shiratamako rice flour
⅓ cup + 1 tbsp water
Pink, purple, yellow, green, and orange food
    coloring

Syrup:

½ cup coconut cream
1 tsp. freshly grated ginger
1½ tbsp. light brown sugar
Cheesecloth
Crushed peanuts
Mint leaves

1. First, make the dumplings. Place the rice flour into a bowl, and gradually add the water. Knead with a spoon until the dough forms into one piece, and is firm enough for a piece of dough to be rolled into a ball and retain its form when placed down. Depending on the humidity of your environment, you may need to add a bit more flour or water, but do so very gradually.

2. Divide the dough into 6 portions and roll into balls. Dye them pink, purple, yellow, green, and orange, leaving the remaining ball uncolored.

3. Divide each ball in half and shape them into hearts. If the dough feels crumbly, wet your hands with water and continue to knead.

4. Place the dumplings in a pot of boiling water. Once they have risen to the surface, boil for 1 minute, then place in a bowl of ice water. Transfer to a plate lined with plastic wrap while you make the syrup.

5. To make the syrup, place the coconut cream, ginger, and brown sugar into a pan and bring to a boil. Pour into a bowl lined with cheesecloth to remove any pieces of ginger.

6. Place some crushed peanuts into the bottom of two bowls, and top with the heart dumplings. Then spoon over the coconut syrup, top with a mint leaf and some more crushed peanuts. Enjoy!

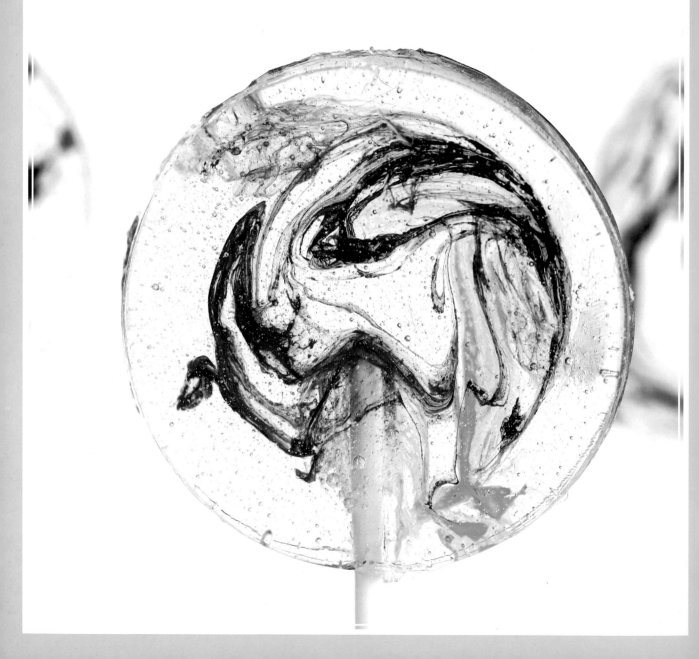

RAINBOW LOLLIPOPS

These beautiful, swirly lollipops are like an edible piece of art! Serve these at your next cocktail party for a colorful, sweet ending to the evening. The quantity of lollipops this recipe makes will depend on the size of mold you use.

2½ cups granulated sugar
1 cup water
1½ cups light corn syrup
Your desired flavoring
Cooking spray
Red, yellow, green, and blue food colouring
Lollipop sticks

1. Place a pot over medium heat and add the granulated sugar, water, and light corn syrup. Stir with a rubber spatula until everything is melted and combined. Then increase the heat to medium-high, and attach a candy thermometer to the pot. Heat the sugar until it reaches 310°F.

2. Remove the pot from the heat and stir until it stops bubbling. Add the flavoring and mix until fully combined.

3. Generously spray a lollipop mold with cooking spray. Working with one mold at a time, pour some candy into the mold. Dip a toothpick in some food coloring and swirl it in the hot candy, creating a rainbow pattern. Insert a lollipop stick. Repeat with the remaining hot candy, returning the pot to the heat if the candy starts to thicken and cool.

4. Allow the lollipops to cool at room temperature until fully hardened, about 1 hour.

5. Unmold and enjoy!

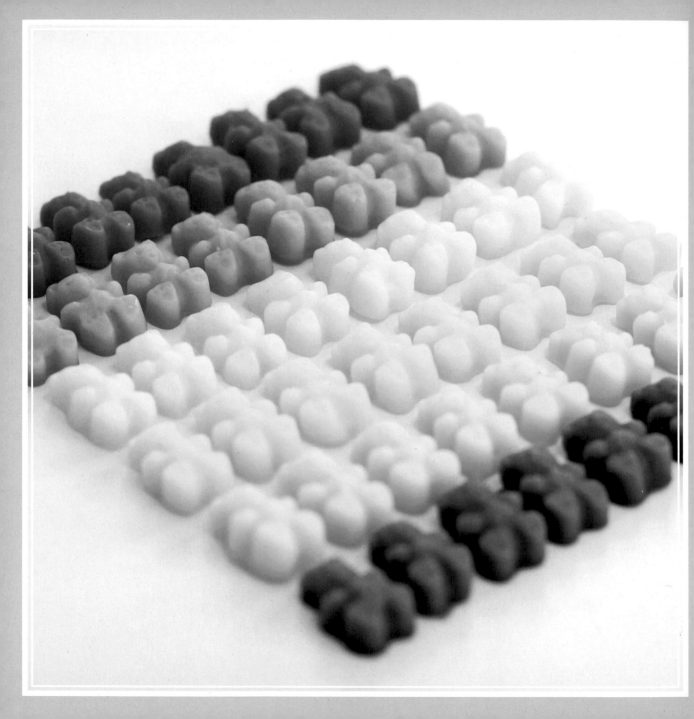

Rainbow Gummy Bears

These beautiful pastel gummy bears are the perfect treat for movie night, or for decorating cupcakes!

1 cup cold water
½ cup powdered gelatin
1 cup sweetened condensed milk
¼ cup sugar
Pink, orange, yellow, green, blue, and purple
    food coloring
Your desired flavoring (we used watermelon,
    mango, pineapple, key lime, cake batter,
    and raspberry)

1. Pour the cold water into a pot and add the gelatin. Allow the gelatin to develop for 5 minutes. Set the pot to medium heat and whisk constantly until the gelatin has melted and is liquid.

2. Add the sweetened condensed milk and sugar and whisk until fully combined.

3. Remove from the heat and divide the mixture into 6 bowls. Dye each a color of the rainbow and add a small drop of your desired flavoring to each color.

4. Pour the gummy bears into a gummy bear mold and place in the fridge until set, about 1 hour. Unmold and enjoy!

Rainbow Vanilla Pudding

This vanilla pudding is smooth and creamy and very simple to whip up! No need to use store-bought pudding again!

3 tbsp. cornstarch
½ cup granulated sugar
Pinch salt
2 large egg yolks
½ cup heavy cream
1½ cups milk
1 vanilla bean pod, seeds only
2 tbsp. unsalted butter, cold and cut into cubes
Pink, orange, yellow, green, blue, and purple
   food coloring

TIP: *For a dairy-free version, use coconut cream instead of milk!*

1. Pour the cornstarch, sugar, and salt into a pot. Whisk to combine. Add the egg yolks and heavy cream and whisk until well-combined. Add the milk and mix well.

2. Set the pot to medium-high heat and whisk constantly for 5–10 minutes, until the mixture has thickened and is bubbling.

3. Pour the pudding through a sieve, then add the vanilla bean seeds and butter, whisking until well-combined.

4. Press a sheet of plastic wrap onto the surface of the pudding and place in the fridge until chilled, about 3 hours. If the pudding becomes lumpy, place in a food processor and pulse 2–3 times, until smooth.

5. Divide the pudding into 6 bowls and dye them the colors of the rainbow.

Mosaic Jellies

Rainbows glisten from within condensed milk jelly!

½ package (1½ oz.) each of red, orange, yellow,
   green, blue, and purple Jell-O powder
3 cups + ¾ cup boiling water
¼ cup cold water
1 tbsp. powdered gelatin
½ 14-oz. can sweetened condensed milk

1. Divide each Jell-O flavor into a separate bowl and pour ½ cup of boiling water into each bowl. Whisk until the Jell-O has completely dissolved and transfer to the fridge until fully set, about 2 hours.

2. Unmold the jellies and cut into cubes. Set aside.

3. Pour ¼ cup cold water into a large bowl and sprinkle the powdered gelatin on top. Let sit for 5 minutes. Add ¾ cup boiling water and mix well. Add the condensed milk and mix until fully combined. Allow to cool slightly.

4. Line a 7x4-inch dish with plastic wrap. Place half of the jelly cubes into the dish and pour half of the condensed milk mixture on top. Place in the fridge until the jelly is partially set, then top with the remaining jelly cubes and condensed milk mixture. Refrigerate for 2–3 hours, or until fully set.

5. Remove the jelly block from the dish, slice into your desired shapes, and enjoy!

Edible Unicorn Horns

These horns can be enjoyed on their own, or used as a decoration for cakes, cupcakes, or any sweet treat!

You will need 5 sets of the following ingredients, one each for red, orange, yellow, green, and blue. So you will need 5 total packs of Jell-O in different colors, 3 tablespoons soda for each color, etc.

Per color:
½ package Jell-O powder (so you will need 5 total packs of Jell-O, 1 for each color)
3 tbsp. Sprite, or any clear soda
1¼ cups confectioner's sugar
Food coloring, if desired

1. Using only your first set of ingredients, combine the Jell-O powder and clear soda in a microwave-safe bowl and microwave for 30 seconds, or until the Jell-O has completely dissolved.

2. Place 1¼ cups of confectioner's sugar in a large bowl and add the Jell-O mixture. Mix with an electric mixer until fully combined. The confectioner's sugar will lighten the color of the Jell-O, so if desired, add a couple drops of food coloring at this point to create a more vibrant color.

3. Gradually add the remaining confectioner's sugar until the dough is malleable and no longer sticky. If the dough cracks and is too dry, add a couple extra drops of soda.

4. Dust your work surface with extra confectioner's sugar and knead the dough several times. Wrap the dough tightly in plastic wrap to prevent it from drying out.

5. Using your 4 remaining batches of ingredients, repeat to create red, orange, yellow, green, and blue dough.

6. Tear off about 1 tbsp. from each ball of dough, wrapping the remaining dough in plastic wrap. Roll the pieces of dough into long sausages and line them up in the order of the rainbow. Press them together, then slowly twist them together to create a spiral pattern.

7. Trim the top and edges to create a clean shape, then place on a baking sheet lined with parchment paper. Repeat with the remaining dough to make each unicorn horn. Leave the horns at room temperature for 24 hours until they have dried out and hardened. Enjoy!

DRINKS

Unicorn Dust Milkshake

Dream of vanilla swirls and pastels as you sip on this delicious vanilla milkshake!

2½ cups vanilla ice cream
¾–1 cup milk
Pink, purple, and blue food coloring
Whipped cream
Pink, purple, and blue sprinkles
Golden sprinkles
Yellow star sprinkles

1. Divide the ice cream and milk into 3 equal portions. Place ⅓ of the ice cream and ⅓ of the milk at a time in a blender, and add a drop of either pink, blue, or purple food coloring. Repeat with the remaining two portions, so you have 3 different colors.

2. Layer the 3 colors in tall glasses. Using more milk will create a swirly pattern, while less milk will create more distinct lines between the colors.

3. Top with some whipped cream and sprinkles and enjoy!

Rainbow Champagne Jellies

Perfect for a cocktail party or a playful treat for a movie night in.

1 cup (16 packets) powdered gelatin
2 cups water
6 cups champagne + extra for filling the glasses
Pink, orange, yellow, green, blue, and purple food coloring

1. Sprinkle the gelatin into the water and allow the gelatin to develop for 5 minutes.

2. Transfer the gelatin to a pot and set to medium heat. Whisk constantly until it has completely melted and is liquid. Add the champagne and whisk well to combine.

3. Divide the mixture into 6 bowls and dye each one a color of the rainbow. Place the bowls in the fridge and chill until the jelly has completely set.

4. Break each color of jelly into large pieces and pulse in a food processor until it resembles shaved ice.

5. Spoon the jellies into champagne glasses, layering them in the order of the rainbow.

6. Slowly fill the glasses with extra champagne. Enjoy!

FRESH FRUIT FRAPPE

Treat yourself to a refreshing frappe topped with delicious fresh fruit.

2 cups ice
1 cup vanilla ice cream
1 cup milk
Fresh fruit, chopped into bite-sized pieces
   (strawberries, kiwi, peaches, mandarin
   oranges)
Freshly whipped cream
Fresh mint leaves

1. Place the ice, vanilla ice cream, and milk in a blender and pulse until smooth.

2. Pour the mixture into two tall glasses, and top with a thin layer of freshly whipped cream. Top with any fresh fruit that you like, then top with more whipped cream and garnish with a mint leaf.

Rainbow Make-Ahead Cocktails

Hosting a dinner party is never complete without rushing around thirty minutes before guests arrive. These cocktails will be your savior! Make them the night before, pop them into the fridge, and rest easy knowing that you'll have refreshments ready for your guests the moment they arrive! The trick is in the ice—as it melts, the layers separate to create a beautiful rainbow gradient.

Ice cubes

Red layer:

4 oz. grenadine
4 cups ice

Orange layer:

3 oz. pineapple juice
1 oz. grenadine

Yellow layer:

2 oz. pineapple juice
2 oz. lemonade
2 oz. triple sec

Green layer:

4 oz. Midori
3 oz. lemonade
1 oz. vodka

Blue layer:

4 oz. vodka
2 oz. blue curaçao

1. Divide the grenadine (red layer) between all 8 glasses.

2. Fill the glasses ¾ full with ice.

3. Combine the ingredients for each remaining layer in small cups, then divide them between the glasses, working in the order of the rainbow. To maintain clean lines, tilt the glasses slightly to the side and slowly pour the liquid along the sides of the glasses.

4. Transfer the drinks to the fridge to chill for 6 hours, or until the ice has melted.

5. Remove them from the fridge to reveal the beautiful rainbow layers!

Unicorn Hot Chocolate

Creamy white hot chocolate is topped with a candy unicorn horn and ears to create a whimsical drink, perfect for sweater weather!

3 pink candy chews
3 yellow candy chews
Silver Luster Dust
2 jumbo marshmallows
Pink sugar
3 oz. white chocolate
2 cups milk
Whipped cream
Mini marshmallows
Rainbow sprinkles

Toppings:

1. To make the horns, separate the pink and yellow candy chews into individual microwave-safe dishes. Microwave for 10–15 seconds, until just melted and malleable. Once they have cooled just enough to handle, roll both colors into 2 thin logs each, then twist a pink and yellow strand together and shape into a horn. Repeat with the remaining pink and yellow candy logs. Use a clean paintbrush to coat the unicorn horns with silver Luster Dust. Set aside.

2. To make the ears, slice the jumbo marshmallows in half diagonally with scissors. Dip the sticky sides into pink sugar. Set aside.

Make the hot chocolate:

1. Place the white chocolate and milk into a small pot, set to low heat, and stir until the milk is hot and the chocolate has fully melted.

2. Pour into 2 mugs and top with some whipped cream, mini marshmallows, and rainbow sprinkles. Place 2 ears on top and mold the candy unicorn horns to rest on the edges of the mugs. Enjoy!

Rainbow Candy Shot Glasses

A fun touch to add to any party! The contents of the shot glasses will gradually take on the flavor of the candies you used, so be creative! Strawberry candies will create strawberry-flavored vodka, and so on.

Approx. 5 cups Rainbow Hard Candies
   (page 79)

TIP: *For a festive touch, use broken candy canes or peppermint hard candies! Butterscotch hard candies would also be delicious served with Irish liqueur.*

1. Pack the hard candies into a silicone shot glass mold in 2 layers. Place 1 or 2 candies on top, to create the base of the shot glasses. Do not worry if the mold is bulging—the candies will melt in the oven, bend to shape the mold, and fill in any open gaps between the candies.

2. Place the silicone mold on a baking sheet and bake at 375°F for 15 minutes, or until the candy has completely melted.

3. Transfer the entire baking sheet to a cooling rack and allow the candies to cool completely, about 1 hour. Then unmold and reveal your homemade shot glasses!

4. Shot glasses should be stored at room temperature.

RAINBOW BUBBLE PUNCH

Quench your thirst with a bubbly rainbow!

Red bubbles:

⅓ cup water
4 tbsp. powdered gelatin
1 cup red cranberry juice

Yellow bubbles:

⅓ cup water
4 tbsp. powdered gelatin
1 cup orange juice

Green bubbles:

⅓ cup water
4 tbsp. powdered gelatin
½ cup fresh lime juice
½ cup lemon lime soda
Green food coloring

Blue bubbles:

⅓ cup water
4 tbsp. powdered gelatin
½ cup fresh lemon juice
½ cup lemon lime soda
Blue food coloring

Punch:

6 cups white grape juice
2 cups lemon lime soda
2 cups white cranberry juice

To make the bubbles:

1. Follow the same steps to create each separate color of bubble: Pour the water into a microwave-safe bowl and sprinkle the gelatin on top. Microwave for 30 seconds, until the gelatin has fully dissolved.

2. Combine the juice, soda, and food coloring (if using) in a bowl. Add the gelatin mixture and whisk until combined.

3. Pour the liquid into a 1-inch sphere-shaped mold and place in the fridge until fully set, about 30 minutes.

To serve:

1. Pour the white grape juice, lemon lime soda, and white cranberry juice into a large pitcher or punch bowl.

2. Right before serving, unmold the bubbles and add them to the punch. Enjoy!

Peppermint Frozen Hot Chocolate

How about a frozen hot chocolate for a change during the holidays? It's just like a milkshake, but with a melted chocolate swirl!

3 oz. white chocolate, melted (+ extra for
    decorating the glass)
4 candy canes, crushed
3 tbsp. warm milk
2 cups candy cane ice cream (or mint
    chocolate chip ice cream)
½ cup cold milk
Whipped cream
Whole candy canes
Festive straws

1. First, decorate the glasses. Drizzle some white chocolate onto the inside of 2 chilled glasses. Spread some melted white chocolate along the rims. Immediately sprinkle some crushed candy canes onto the chocolate rims and place them in the freezer for the chocolate to set while you make the drink.

2. In a small bowl, combine the melted 3 oz. white chocolate and warm milk. Add this to a blender along with some candy cane ice cream and cold milk. Blend until smooth.

3. Pour into the glasses and top with some whipped cream and extra crushed candy canes. Garnish with a full candy cane and festive straw. Enjoy!

RAINBOW SANGRIA

A beautiful and refreshing way to enjoy warmer weather! Fruit is stacked high in glasses and steeped with delicious white wine sangria.

25-oz. bottle of white wine
3 tbsp. sugar
1 cup strawberries, quartered
1 cup pineapple, cubed
3 kiwis, peeled and sliced
½ cup blackberries
½ cup raspberries
25-oz. bottle of Prosecco

1. Pour the white wine and sugar into a large pitcher and stir to combine. Add the fruit, except for the blackberries and raspberries, then place in the fridge and chill for 1 hour. Add the blackberries, raspberries, and Prosecco, and stir to combine.

2. Spoon the fruit into glasses, arranging the fruit in the order of the rainbow.

3. Pour the sangria into the glasses. Enjoy!

Chocolate Egg Hot Chocolate

These chocolate eggs are filled with rich ganache and when dropped into hot milk, melt into delicious hot chocolate!

8 oz. chocolate (milk, white, or dark), melted
½ cup whipping cream, hot
Cooking spray or plastic wrap
1 cup chocolate chips, melted
2 tbsp. coconut oil, melted
Colorful meltable candy discs, melted (any color you like)

1. Combine the melted chocolate and whipping cream in a bowl. Spoon the mixture into an egg-shaped mold that is either sprayed with cooking spray or lined with plastic wrap. Place the eggs in the freezer until stiff, about 1–2 hours.

2. Unmold the eggs (if they are stuck, try gently releasing them with a sharp knife). Transfer them to a plate lined with plastic wrap and return to the freezer.

3. Combine the melted chocolate chips and liquid coconut oil. Place an egg on a fork and submerge in the coating. Run the bottom of the fork against the rim of the bowl to remove any excess chocolate, then return to the plate. Repeat with the remaining eggs and place them in the freezer.

4. Place the melted candies into piping bags fitted with #3 round piping tips and drizzle them onto the eggs.

5. To serve, dunk one egg into 1 cup hot milk and stir until fully melted. For extra chocolately hot chocolate, add an extra egg!

Unicorn Mug Toppers

Decorate your mug of coffee or tea with these cute unicorn cookies!

Cookie dough:

2 cups flour
¼ tsp. salt
½ tsp. baking powder
Pinch ground cinnamon
¼ cup confetti sprinkles
½ cup unsalted butter
1 cup sugar
2 tbsp. milk
1 large egg
½ tsp vanilla extract

Royal icing:

½ lb. confectioner's sugar
2½ tbsp. meringue powder
Scant ¼ cup water
Pink, yellow, green, blue, and purple food coloring
1 tsp. vodka or any clear flavoring
Gold Luster Dust
Edible ink pens

Make the cookies:

1. Mix dry ingredients and sprinkles in a bowl. In a separate bowl, cream the butter and sugar with an electric mixer until it becomes light and fluffy. Add last 3 ingredients, and mix well. Then slowly add the flour mixture until it is just combined.

2. Shape the dough into a ball, then divide it in half. Wrap each ball in plastic wrap and place in the refrigerator for 1 hour.

3. Roll the dough out until ¼ inch thick and cut into unicorn shapes with a unicorn cookie cutter. Transfer to a baking sheet lined with parchment paper. Cut out ½ inch long notches between the unicorns' necks and manes. This should be slightly wider than the thickness of the mug you will be using, because the space will narrow slightly during baking. Bake the cookies at 350°F for 10 minutes, or until the edges are just starting to brown. Transfer to a wire rack and cool completely.

Make the royal icing:

1. Combine sugar and meringue powder in a large bowl. Add the water and beat for 7 minutes, until it is smooth, and when drizzled stays on the surface for a few seconds.

2. Divide the icing in half into 2 bowls. Press some plastic wrap onto the surface of one bowl and set aside. Divide the remaining icing into 5 bowls and dye them pink, yellow, green, blue, and purple. Press plastic wrap onto the surface of each bowl of icing. Set aside.

Decorate the cookies:

1. Place ½ of the white icing into a piping bag fitted with a #3 round piping tip. Pipe a border around the head and neck portion of the cookies.

2. Add about 2 teaspoons of water to the remaining white icing to create a thinner consistency. Use a

continued on page 122

small spoon to fill in the outlined portion of the cookies with the thin white icing. Allow to fully harden at room temperature, about 1 hour.

3. Place the pink, yellow, green, blue, and purple icing into individual piping bags fitted with #3 round piping tips.

4. Pipe the horn with the yellow icing. Then pipe the mane by making curls with the other colors. Allow the icing to fully harden at room temperature, about 1 hour.

5. Dip a clean paintbrush into the gold Luster Dust and brush onto the unicorn's horn. Draw the unicorn's eyes, nostrils, and mouths with the edible ink pens.

6. Hook the cookies onto the mugs and enjoy with your favorite hot drink!

Frozen Treats

Gummy Bear Ice Pops

A simple, sweet, and fun treat. The gummy bears glow from the inside and are a guaranteed hit with kids!

½ cup gummy bears
1½ cups aloe juice or any juice you like

1. Fill your ice pop mold with gummy bears in a variety of colors. Pour the juice into the mold and top with popsicle sticks.

2. Place in the freezer for 5 hours or until completely frozen.

3. To unmold, run the mold under hot water for 5–10 seconds. Gently pull the pops out and enjoy!

Lucky Charms Ice Cream Cones

These are a much more delicious option than traditional ice cream cones!

3 tbsp. unsalted butter

40 large marshmallows (or 4 cups mini marshmallows)

6 cups Lucky Charms cereal

> **TIP:** *If you're not a fan of Lucky Charms cereal, use any cereal that you like!*

1. Set a pan to medium heat and add the butter. Once the butter has melted, add the marshmallows and mix until fully melted. Remove from the heat and add the Lucky Charms cereal. Mix until fully combined.

2. Spray a cookie sheet with cooking spray and turn the cereal out onto the sheet. Use a rubber spatula to flatten out the cereal as much as possible. Allow to cool completely.

3. Slice the Lucky Charms mixture into triangles with a sharp knife. Spray your hands with cooking spray and shape the triangles into cones.

4. Place the cones on a plate lined with wax paper and freeze until stiff, about 10–20 minutes. Then fill with ice cream and enjoy!

RAINBOW SEMI-FREDDO

This is a creamy, sliceable ice cream dessert and is a perfect treat after a summertime barbecue dinner.

6 large egg yolks
½ cup sugar
1½ cups whipping cream
1¼ cups white chocolate, melted and cooled to
  room temperature
Pink, orange, yellow, green, blue, and purple
  food coloring
Whipped cream
Mini rainbow marshmallows
Confetti sprinkles

1. Place a heatproof bowl over a pot of simmering water. Add the egg yolks and sugar and whisk for 2 minutes, until thickened and lightened in color.

2. Pour into a bowl set in an ice bath and chill for 30 minutes.

3. Pour the whipping cream into a separate bowl and beat with an electric mixer until soft peaks form. Add this to the chilled mixture and fold to combine. Add the melted white chocolate and gently fold to combine.

4. Divide the mixture into 5 bowls and dye them pink, orange, yellow, green, blue, and purple with food coloring, folding very gently to combine.

5. Line a 7x4-inch container with plastic wrap, with extra plastic wrap hanging off the sides. Pour the pink layer into the container and smooth the surface. Place in the freezer until stiff, about 30 minutes. Store the remaining layers in the fridge in the meantime. Pour the orange layer on top, smooth the surface, return to the freezer, and freeze until stiff. Repeat with the remaining layers, working in the order of the rainbow. Once all layers have been added, fold the excess plastic wrap onto the surface and freeze for 3–4 hours, or until it is very stiff.

6. Peel the plastic wrap off the surface and invert onto a plate. Remove the remaining plastic wrap. Top with whipped cream, mini marshmallows, and confetti sprinkles. Enjoy!

Rainbow Smoothie Pops

These pops are so creamy and delicious and are a wonderful breakfast for hot, summer days.

Red layer:

½ banana
¼ cup vanilla yogurt
¼ cup frozen raspberries
¼ cup frozen strawberries
Sliced strawberries for garnish

Yellow layer:

½ banana
¼ cup vanilla yogurt
¼ cup frozen peaches
½ fresh orange
Golden raspberries for garnish

White layer:

½ banana
¼ cup vanilla yogurt
½ cup canned pineapple chunks

Green layer:

½ banana
¼ cup vanilla yogurt
½ cup canned pineapple chunks
1 small handful spinach leaves

Purple layer:

½ banana
¼ cup vanilla yogurt
¼ cup fresh blueberries + extra for garnish
¼ cup fresh blackberries + extra for garnish

1. Working layer by layer, pulse all ingredients for each layer, except those used for garnish, in a blender until very smooth. Pour into a small bowl and repeat with the remaining layers.

2. Gently spoon the layers into a mold, adding the ingredients for garnish after pouring in the mixture for the corresponding layer. Slide a wooden craft stick into each mold and freeze for 4–6 hours, or until completely frozen.

3. To unmold, run the base of the molds under warm water, then gently wiggle the sticks to loosen the popsicles from the mold. To store, wrap each pop in wax paper, then place them all in a freezer bag and store in the freezer. Enjoy!

Rainbow No-Churn Ice Cream

This ice cream is so smooth and creamy with a wonderful vanilla flavor.

1¾ cup whipping cream
Pink, orange, yellow, green, blue, and purple
   food coloring
4 large eggs
⅔ cup sugar
1 tsp. vanilla extract

TIP: *Keeping the mixture as airy as possible when mixing is going to give the finished ice cream a very creamy and smooth texture.*

1. Beat the whipping cream with an electric mixer until it forms a thick ribbon when the whisk is lifted. Divide the cream into 6 bowls and add a different shade of food coloring to each bowl. Very gently fold to combine. Place the cream in the fridge.

2. In a separate bowl, whisk the eggs then add the sugar and vanilla. Beat well with an electric mixer until the mixture forms a ribbon when the whisk is lifted and the ribbon remains on the surface of the mixture for a few seconds.

3. Divide the egg mixture between the rainbow whipped cream and gently fold the mixture together to combine. Make sure to be gentle and keep the mixture as airy as possible.

4. Dollop the ice cream into a plastic container to create a rainbow pattern, and seal with the lid. Place this in the freezer for 7–8 hours to chill and set. Enjoy!

Rainbow Hard-Crack Ice Cream Shell

Just like the dipped ice cream you can buy at the ice cream shop, but rainbow!

6 oz. high quality white chocolate
2 tbsp. coconut oil, melted
Oil-based food coloring, any color

> **TIP:** *If you're not a fan of white chocolate, you can substitute dark or milk chocolate!*

1. Combine the white chocolate and liquid coconut oil in a microwave-safe bowl and microwave for 30-second intervals until the chocolate has melted. Stir to combine.

2. Divide into as many bowls as you like and dye the chocolate with oil-based food coloring.

3. Pour over some ice cream and watch as the cold temperature of the ice cream turns the chocolate mixture into a hard shell!

Unicorn Parfaits

Indulge yourself in spoonfuls of rainbow, marshmallow, and sweetness!

2 cups strawberry ice cream
1 cup marshmallow cream
1 cup chocolate ice cream
2 scoops Rainbow No-Churn Ice Cream
    (page 133)
Fresh fruit (we used mango, strawberries,
    and kiwi)
Rainbow sprinkles
Rock candy

1. Fill parfait glasses ⅓ of the way full with strawberry ice cream.

2. Place the marshmallow into a piping bag fitted with a large, round piping tip and pipe clouds onto the insides of the glasses.

4. Spoon some chocolate ice cream into the glasses, filling them ⅔ of the way full. Repeat with more marshmallow clouds and strawberry ice cream, until the glasses are full.

5. Top with the remaining marshmallow fluff and decorate with a scoop of Rainbow No-Churn Ice Cream, fresh fruit, rainbow sprinkles, and rock candy. Enjoy!

Watermelon Shaved Ice

This is a simple technique to turn melon into shaved ice, without the need of any fancy equipment!

Watermelon granita:

1⅔ tsp. powdered gelatin

¼ cup water

2¼ cups watermelon (about 1 small watermelon), pureed in a blender (note: slice the watermelon in half, scoop out the flesh, and save the rind for later)

6½ tbsp. sugar

⅓ cup water

Honeydew granita:

1⅔ tsp. powdered gelatin

¼ cup water

2¼ cups honeydew melon, pureed in a blender

6½ tbsp. sugar

⅓ cup water

1 tbsp. mini chocolate chips

1. For the watermelon granita, sprinkle the gelatin into ¼ cup water in a microwave-safe dish and set aside.

2. Place the watermelon into a freezer bag and pour in the sugar and ⅓ cup of water.

3. Microwave the gelatin mixture from step 1 in the microwave for 30 seconds on high heat. Pour the mixture into the freezer bag with the watermelon and mix well. Repeat all steps to make the honeydew granita.

4. Place the freezer bags into the freezer for 2–4 hours, kneading the bags occasionally until the contents develop a granita-like texture.

5. Divide the honeydew granita between the 2 hollowed out watermelon halves, then top with the watermelon granita. Sprinkle some mini chocolate chips on top and enjoy!

Unicorn Banana Pops

These are a cute, healthier alternative to traditional sweet treats. Bananas develop a very similar texture to ice cream when frozen, so these will hit the spot without the guilt!

3 fresh bananas, peeled and cut in half
6 lollipop sticks
½ cup strawberry yogurt
Pink food coloring
½ cup dark chocolate, melted
½ cup white chocolate, melted
Rainbow sprinkles

1. Skewer the banana halves onto the lollipop sticks and arrange on a small baking sheet lined with parchment paper.

2. Add a couple drops of pink food coloring to the strawberry yogurt to create a vibrant pink color. Alternate dipping the bananas in dark chocolate, white chocolate, and yogurt, and return to the baking sheet.

3. To decorate, sprinkle the entire surface of the bananas with sprinkles and place them in the freezer until the coating has fully set, about 15–20 minutes. For a drizzled look, place the bananas into the freezer after dipping them in the coating for about 15–20 minutes. Once the coating has set, drizzle the bananas with a coating in a contrasting color and sprinkle with sprinkles. Return the bananas to the freezer until the drizzle has set, about 10 minutes.

4. To store, wrap each banana in wax paper, then place all bananas in a freezer bag. Enjoy the bananas one by one, or serve by the pool on a hot day!

Breakfast Treats

Rainbow Bagels

There is nothing like freshly baked bagels, especially when they're rainbow! These bagels are so light and fluffy and taste delicious with cream cheese!

2¼ cups warm water, divided
2¼ tsp active dry yeast
2 tbsp. sugar
3 tbsp. vegetable shortening
1 tbsp. salt
6 cups bread flour
2 tbsp. melted butter
½–1 tsp each of pink, orange, yellow, green, blue, and purple gel food coloring
¼ cup sugar
1 tsp. baking soda
Cooking spray
Sesame seeds
2 large egg whites
1 tsp. cold water
4 ice cubes
¼ cup water

1. Pour ¼ cup of warm water into the bowl of an electric mixer and sprinkle the yeast on top. Let sit for 5 minutes for the yeast to develop. Add the remaining 2 cups warm water, sugar, vegetable shortening, and salt, and mix on low speed with a dough hook attachment.

2. Gradually add 5 ½ cups of bread flour, mixing for 2–3 minutes until all ingredients are combined. Increase to medium speed and mix for 6 minutes, adding the remaining flour 1 tablespoon at a time.

3. Brush the inside of a large bowl with some of the melted butter. Shape the dough into a ball and place inside the bowl. Brush the top of the ball with some more butter and cover with a sheet of buttered plastic wrap. Place a towel on top and let the dough rise at room temperature for 1 hour.

4. Transfer the dough to a floured surface and divide into 6 even portions. Dye each portion a different color with the gel food coloring. It will take a few minutes for the food coloring to evenly disperse throughout the dough, but keep kneading and you will eventually have a smooth, even color. (TIP: Wipe down your countertop and wash your hands in between colors, to prevent any color transfer. To further prevent this, dye the dough in this order: yellow > orange > pink > purple > blue > green.)

5. Place each ball of dough in individual buttered bowls and brush some more butter on top of each ball of dough. Cover with a buttered sheet of plastic wrap and a dish towel and let rise at room temperature for 1 hour and 30 minutes. Then transfer the bowls to the fridge and chill for 1 hour.

6. In the meantime, do some prep. Spray 2 baking sheets with cooking spray and sprinkle sesame seeds on top. Cover 2 additional baking sheets with dish towels and sprinkle flour onto one of the dish towels. Set aside.

7. Transfer the balls of dough to a floured surface one color at a time. Deflate the dough and roll it out into a rectangle shape. Stack the colors of dough in the order of the rainbow (pink > orange > yellow > green > blue > purple). Gently roll the dough out a little to seal the colors together, then

continued on page 146

divide the dough in half. Wrap one half in buttered plastic wrap and return to the fridge. Slice the remaining half into 5 pieces, then roll them into sausage shapes. Twist them once or twice to create a swirly pattern, then shape them into rings by pinching the ends together. Transfer the bagels to the baking sheet with the floured dish towel and cover with an additional dish towel.

8. Bring a large pot of water to boil and add the sugar and baking soda. Place the bagels into the boiling water and boil for 1½–2 minutes, then flip over and boil for an additional 1½–2 minutes on the other side. Transfer the boiled bagels to the baking sheet lined with the un-floured dish towel. Then transfer the bagels to one of the baking sheets sprinkled with sesame seeds.

9. Preheat the oven to 500°F. While the oven is preheating, beat the egg whites and water in a small bowl. Brush the bagels with this glaze, and if desired, sprinkle with additional sesame seeds. Place a sheet of aluminum foil over the bagels (this will prevent them from browning and will maintain the bright rainbow color).

10. Place 4 ice cubes and ¼ cup water in a small glass. Place the bagels in the oven and immediately toss the ice cubes and water onto the oven floor. This will create a burst of steam in the oven, which contributes to the bagels' delicious crust. Quickly close the oven door and reduce the oven temperature to 450°F. Bake for 25 minutes. Turn off the oven and keep the bagels in the oven for an additional 5 minutes. Then open the oven door and leave the bagels in the oven for an additional 5 minutes. While the first batch is baking, prep the other bagels using the remaining dough.

11. After cooking, transfer the bagels to a cooling rack and enjoy!

Rainbow Cinnamon Rolls

These cinnamon rolls are so buttery, flaky, and indulgent! Make them as a special treat for brunch and try to stop at just one!

Brioche:

⅓ cup whole milk, warm
2¼ tsp. active dry yeast
5 eggs
3½ cups all-purpose flour, divided
⅓ cup sugar
1 tsp. salt
1½ cups unsalted butter, room temperature, divided in half
Pink, orange, yellow, green, blue, and purple food coloring

Filling:

6 tbsp. sugar
3½ tsp. cinnamon
1 egg, beaten
¾ cup unsalted butter, room temperature

Icing:

8 oz. cream cheese, room temperature
1½ cups confectioner's sugar
4 tbsp. milk
Rainbow sprinkles

Make the brioche:

1. Pour the milk, yeast, 1 egg, and 1 cup flour into the bowl of an electric mixer. Mix to combine, then sprinkle over another 1 cup flour. Let rise for 40 minutes.

2. Add the remaining 4 eggs to the dough along with the sugar, salt, and 1 more cup flour. Place these into a mixer fitted with a dough hook and mix on low speed for 2 minutes. Add the remaining ½ cup flour and mix on medium speed for 15 minutes.

3. Reduce the speed to medium-low and gradually add ¾ cup butter. Increase the speed to medium-high and beat for 1 minute, then reduce the speed to medium and beat for 5 minutes.

4. Place the dough in a large, buttered bowl and cover with plastic wrap. Let rise for 2½ hours.

5. Deflate the dough, then divide into 6 pieces. Dye them pink, orange, yellow, green, blue, and purple. It may take some time for the food coloring to evenly disperse through the dough, but don't give up! It will happen. Place the balls of dough on a buttered baking sheet and cover with plastic wrap. Let sit for 4–6 hours, or up to overnight.

6. Divide each ball of dough in half. Set one of each color of dough aside. Roll the other 6 balls of dough into 10-inch-long logs, then arrange them side by side on a floured surface, pinching the edges together

continued on page 149

to create one large piece of dough. Roll the dough into an 11x13-inch rectangle. Evenly disperse half of the remaining butter onto the surface of the dough, then fold the dough into thirds, like a letter.

7. Roll the dough out into an 11x13-inch rectangle, then fold into thirds again. Wrap tightly in plastic wrap and place in the fridge for 30 minutes. Repeat with the remaining dough.

8. Combine the sugar and cinnamon in a bowl and set aside.

9. Place one piece of dough on a floured surface and roll into an 11x13-inch rectangle. Brush the surface with the beaten egg. Sprinkle half of the cinnamon sugar onto the dough, leaving the top quarter of the dough bare. Roll the dough into a log, starting with the cinnamon sugar end and ending with the bare end. Wrap in plastic wrap and place in the freezer for 45 minutes. Repeat with the remaining dough. (Note: if you are making this for a party or a brunch, you can complete the previous steps a day in advance and start from Step 10 on the day you are serving them.)

10. Divide ¾ cup butter between two 9-inch round baking tins.

11. Unwrap the logs and slice them into 1½-inch-thick buns, making 14 buns. Place 7 buns in each tin. Let the buns rise at room temperature for 1½ hours.

12. Bake the buns at 350°F for 35–40 minutes, until golden brown. Place a baking sheet lined with parchment paper on the rack under the cinnamon buns to catch any drips.

13. As soon as the cinnamon buns are finished baking, flip them out onto a wire rack. Excess butter may drip out, so make sure to place some paper towel under the rack. Turn the buns right side up, and let slightly cool.

14. To make the icing, place the cream cheese in a bowl and beat with an electric mixer for 2 minutes, until the cream cheese is fluffy. Add the confectioner's sugar and milk and beat until combined.

15. Drizzle the icing on top of the cinnamon buns, then decorate with sprinkles.

Rainbow French Toast

Slice into this French toast to reveal rainbow ribbons of cream cheese inside! If you're feeling indulgent this weekend, this is the perfect brunch treat!

½ loaf of egg bread, crusts removed
8 oz. cream cheese, room temperature
Pink, orange, yellow, green, blue, and purple
    food coloring
3 large eggs
A few drops vanilla extract
Pinch ground cinnamon
1 cup milk
2 tbsp. butter
¾ cup granulated sugar
1½ tbsp. ground cinnamon
Whipped cream
Rainbow sprinkles

1. Slice the bread into two 2-inch-thick slices. Slice an opening into one side of each slice, creating pockets. Set aside.

2. Divide the cream cheese into 6 bowls and dye each a color of the rainbow. Place each color into its own piping bag and snip off the tips to create a small, round opening. Working in the order of the rainbow, pipe lines of cream cheese into the bread pockets.

3. In a large bowl, beat the eggs until frothy. Add the vanilla extract, cinnamon, and milk, and whisk until combined. Add the bread and soak for 5 minutes on each side.

4. Melt the butter in a large frying pan set to medium heat. Add the bread and cook for 3–4 minutes per side, until golden brown. Turn off the heat and keep the pan on the stove. Place a lid on the pan and allow the toast to steam for 5 minutes. This will cook any residual raw egg and make the French toast taste wonderfully light and fluffy!

5. Combine the granulated sugar and ground cinnamon in a bowl. Add the French toast and coat in the cinnamon sugar.

6. Transfer to a plate and top with whipped cream and rainbow sprinkles.

Confetti Croissants

These croissants are so sweet, crisp, and buttery, and are the perfect breakfast treat!

4½ tsp. dry active yeast
6 tbsp. warm water
¼ cup sugar
2 tsp. salt
4 tbsp. unsalted butter, melted
2 cups milk
5 cups all-purpose flour
2 cups unsalted butter, room temperature
1 cup confetti sprinkles
1 large egg, beaten

1. Place the yeast and warm water in the bowl of a stand mixer. Allow the yeast to develop for about 5–10 minutes, until very foamy.

2. Add the sugar, salt, melted butter, and milk. Attach a dough hook and mix on medium speed until fully combined. Add the flour ½ cup at a time, mixing until the dough becomes sticky and shapes into a ball, about 5 minutes.

3. Transfer the dough to a floured baking sheet and spread out to ½ inch thick. Cover with plastic wrap and chill in the fridge for 1 hour.

4. Combine the remaining 2 cups butter and confetti sprinkles in a bowl. Place the mixture onto the center of a sheet of parchment paper and use a spatula to shape the butter into a 6x8-inch rectangle. Place another sheet of parchment paper on top, then transfer everything to a plate and refrigerate until the butter is cold and stiff, about 1 hour.

5. Place the dough on a floured surface and roll out to a 16x10-inch rectangle, with the short side closest to you. Remove the butter from the parchment paper and place in the center of the dough. Take one short end and fold over the entire surface of the butter, pressing the edges

together to seal. Repeat with the remaining short end of dough, folding over the butter and pressing to seal closed. Roll the dough out into a 16x10-inch rectangle, with a short end facing you. Fold the bottom third of the dough into the center, then fold the top third down. Reshape until the dough is 11x6 inches. Wrap the dough in plastic wrap and place in the fridge for 45 minutes.

6. Roll the dough out on a floured surface to a 16x10-inch rectangle. Fold the bottom third of the dough into the center, then fold the top third down. Wrap the dough in plastic wrap and return to the fridge to chill for 30 minutes. Repeat this process 2 more times—rolling and folding the dough, chilling it for 45 minutes between each process. Once you have folded the dough the final time, wrap the dough in plastic wrap and chill in the fridge for 4 hours, or up to overnight.

7. Slice the dough in half, creating 2 squares. Wrap one square in plastic wrap and place in the fridge while you use the first square of dough. Place the square of dough onto a floured work surface and roll out into a 9x18-inch rectangle. Slice the dough in half lengthwise, then cut into 7–8 triangles. Cut a small slice into the base of each triangle. Roll the triangles into croissant shapes, then gently shape into a crescent shape. Repeat with the remaining dough in the fridge.

8. Place the croissants on a baking sheet, spacing them about 3 inches apart. Cover with a clean dish towel, place in a warm spot, and let rise for 1½ hours.

9. Brush the croissants with the beaten egg. Bake at 425°F for 10 minutes, then cover loosely with aluminum foil and bake for an additional 5 minutes, or until golden brown. Place the baking sheet on a wire rack and cool until warm.

10. Enjoy your freshly baked croissants!

Rainbow Pull-Apart Bread

This bread is the perfect treat for a holiday brunch! Simply pull off pieces of soft, fluffy bread and taste the delicious cinnamon sugar and raisin filling.

Dough:

2¼ tsp. dry active yeast
3 tbsp. warm water
⅓ cup milk
¼ cup unsalted butter, cold
¼ cup water
1 tsp. vanilla extract
3 cups all-purpose flour, divided
¼ cup sugar
½ tsp. salt
2 large eggs
Red, orange, yellow, green, blue, and purple food coloring

Filling:

½ cup sugar
1 tsp. ground cinnamon
2 tbsp. unsalted butter, melted
½ cup raisins

1. Pour the yeast and warm water into the bowl of a stand mixer. Allow the yeast to develop for 5 minutes, until foamy.

2. Place the milk and butter into a small pot and set to medium heat. Heat just until the butter has melted and the milk is warm. Add the water and vanilla extract and mix until combined. Set aside.

3. Pour 2 cups flour, sugar, and salt into the bowl with the yeast mixture. Add the milk mixture. Attach a dough hook attachment and mix until just combined. With the mixer on medium speed, add the eggs and mix for 1 minute. Add the remaining flour and knead for 2 minutes, until sticky.

4. Divide the dough into 6 balls and dye them each a color of the rainbow. Transfer the dough to a buttered baking sheet and cover with plastic wrap. Cover the entire baking sheet with a clean dish towel, place in a warm spot, and allow the dough to double in size, about 1 hour.

5. In the meantime, make the filling. Combine the sugar and cinnamon in a bowl. Set aside.

6. After the dough has doubled in size, knead each ball 1–2 times to deflate them, re-shape into balls, then cover with a clean dish towel and let rise for 5 more minutes.

7. Roll each ball of dough into a sausage shape. On a large sheet of plastic wrap, line up the sausages in the order of the rainbow, pinching the edges together with your fingers to remove any seams. Place the dough on a floured surface, dust the surface with more flour, and roll out to a 12x20-inch rectangle.

8. Brush the entire surface of the dough with the melted butter and scatter the raisins on top, gently rolling the rolling pin on top to press them into the dough. Sprinkle the cinnamon sugar filling evenly over the top. Slice the dough vertically into 6 strips, trying to create one strip of each color. Slice each strip into 6 even squares.

9. Stack the squares vertically in the order of the rainbow, then turn the stack on its side and place into a greased and floured 9x5-inch loaf pan. Cover the loaf pan with a clean dish towel, place in a warm spot, and rise for 30–45 minutes, or until it has risen to double in size.

10. Bake the bread at 350°F for 35–45 minutes, until the top is golden brown. If you find that the dough is browning too quickly, loosely cover the pan with a sheet of aluminum foil. Cool the bread in the pan for 25 minutes.

11. Run a knife along the edges of the bread, then remove from the pan and place on your desired serving dish. Enjoy!

Breakfast Cereal Pops

Have dessert for breakfast! Make pops with your favorite breakfast cereal for a delicately sweet, colorful treat.

2 cups cereal, divided (we used Lucky charms, Froot Loops, and Fruity Pebbles)
2 cups milk
1 large scoop vanilla ice cream, melted
A few drops vanilla extract
Wooden craft sticks

1. In a large bowl, combine 1 cup cereal, milk, vanilla ice cream, and vanilla extract, and mix until well combined. Let the cereal steep in the milk mixture for 15 minutes.

2. Strain the milk mixture to remove the cereal, then fill pop molds ¾ of the way full.

3. Fill the molds the remainder of the way with the fresh cereal, gently pressing down to immerse them in the milk mixture.

4. Insert sticks and place them in the freezer for 4 hours, or until set.

5. To remove, run the mold under hot water, making sure not to wet the actual pops. To store, wrap each individual breakfast pop in wax paper and store them together in a freezer bag.

RAINBOW WAFFLES

Start your day with rainbows, in the shape of crisp, buttery waffles!

2 cups all-purpose flour
2 tbsp. sugar
2 tsp. baking powder
1 tsp. baking soda
½ tsp. salt
2 cups buttermilk
1 tsp. vanilla extract
½ cup unsalted butter, melted and cooled
2 large eggs
Red, orange, yellow, green, blue, and purple food coloring

1. Combine the flour, sugar, baking powder, baking soda, and salt.

2. In a separate bowl, combine the buttermilk, vanilla extract, butter, and eggs. Add the flour and mix until just combined. Divide the batter into 6 bowls and dye them each a color of the rainbow with food coloring.

3. Spray a waffle iron with nonstick cooking spray. Working quickly, spoon about 1 tablespoon of each color of batter into each waffle section. Close the iron and cook for 3–5 minutes, or until they are fully cooked. Transfer to a plate or a cooling rack, and repeat with the remaining batter.

4. Serve with some butter and maple syrup or some Rainbow No-Churn Ice Cream (see page 133). Enjoy!

Confetti Pancakes

These rainbow-filled pancakes are delicious as breakfast in bed, or stacked high for a unique birthday cake!

Pancake batter:

1 cup all-purpose flour
2 tbsp. sugar
2 tsp. baking powder
½ tsp. salt
1 cup milk
2 tbsp. unsalted butter, melted
1 large egg
¼ cup confetti sprinkles + extra for topping
Cooking spray, for frying pan

Glaze:

4 oz. cream cheese, room temperature
¾ cup confectioner's sugar
2 tbsp. milk

Whipped cream
Fresh strawberries, chopped

Make the pancakes:

1. Combine the flour, sugar, baking powder, and salt in a bowl. In a larger bowl, combine the milk, butter, egg, and confetti sprinkles, and whisk until fully combined. Add the dry ingredients and whisk together, but make sure not to overmix. Some lumps are fine!

2. Heat a frying pan over medium heat and spray with cooking spray. Dollop 2–3 spoons of batter onto the frying pan and smooth the surface with the spoon. Cook until the surface of the pancakes begins to bubble, about 1–2 minutes. Flip and cook for an additional 1–2 minutes, or until the surface has browned. Continue with the rest of the batter.

Make the glaze:

1. Beat the cream cheese with an electric mixer until smooth. Add the confectioner's sugar and milk and mix until combined.

To serve:

1. Stack the pancakes and pour the glaze on top. Top with whipped cream, extra sprinkles, and strawberries, and enjoy!

Unicorn Breakfast Calzones

These delicious calzones are filled with a light, fruity ricotta mixture and make the perfect weekend treat.

Filling:

¾ cup ricotta cheese
¼ cup mascarpone cheese
1 large egg yolk
1 tsp. vanilla extract
2 tbsp. confectioner's sugar
½ cup fresh fruit, roughly chopped (+ extra for serving)
12 oz. pizza dough, chilled
1 large egg, beaten

Glaze:

4 oz. cream cheese, room temperature
¾ cup confectioner's sugar
2 tbsp. milk
Pink and yellow food coloring
Rainbow sprinkles

Make the filling:

1. In a large bowl, combine the ricotta, mascarpone, egg yolk, vanilla extract, confectioner's sugar, and fresh fruit.

2. Cover with plastic wrap and chill in the fridge for 30 minutes.

Make the calzones:

1. Divide the pizza dough into 6 pieces and roll each piece into a circle 7 inches in diameter.

2. Spoon some ricotta mixture onto the bottom half of each round. Fold the dough over to create half circles and seal the calzones closed. Seal the edges by pinching them with your fingers.

3. Place the calzones on a baking sheet lined with parchment paper and brush with the beaten egg. Bake at 450°F for 10–15 minutes, or until golden brown. Cool the calzones on the pan for 15 minutes.

Make the glaze:

1. Beat the cream cheese with an electric mixer until smooth. Add the confectioner's sugar and milk and beat until combined.

2. Divide the glaze into 2 bowls and dye one pale pink and one yellow.

To serve:

1. Drizzle the pink and yellow glaze on top of the calzones and sprinkle rainbow sprinkles on top.

2. Serve with extra fresh fruit and enjoy!

Unicorn Banana Bread

This banana bread isn't overly sweet and is incredibly moist. Slice it for breakfast, or serve with Rainbow No-Churn Ice Cream (see page 133) for dessert!

Banana bread:

3 ripe bananas, mashed
6 Tbsp. vegetable oil
½ cup sugar
1 egg
1 tsp. vanilla extract
¼ tsp. salt
1½ cups flour
1 tsp. baking soda
1 tsp. baking powder
½ cup confetti sprinkles

Glaze:

4 oz. cream cheese, room temperature
¾ cup confectioner's sugar
2 tbsp. milk
Pink, blue, and yellow food coloring
Rainbow sprinkles

Make the banana bread:

1. Combine bananas, oil, and sugar. Then add the egg, vanilla, and salt.

2. In a separate bowl, mix the flour, baking soda, and baking powder together and add to the banana mixture. Add the confetti sprinkles and mix until combined.

3. Pour into a greased loaf pan and bake at 350°F for 45 minutes, or until a knife inserted into the center of the loaf comes out clean. Cool in the pan for 10 minutes, then turn out onto a wire rack and cool completely.

Make the glaze:

1. Beat the cream cheese with an electric mixer until smooth. Add the confectioner's sugar and milk and beat until combined.

2. Divide the glaze into 3 bowls and dye them pale pink, blue, and yellow.

To serve:

1. Drizzle all colors of glaze onto the banana bread and top with rainbow sprinkles.

2. Enjoy!

CHOCOLATE

GEODE CHOCOLATE EGGS

These sparkly, ganache-filled chocolate eggs will give a unique twist to your Easter table. Use a variety of colors of rock candy to create a beautiful rainbow of glistening eggs!

8 oz. white chocolate, melted
Pinch of salt
Scant ¾ cup whipping cream, hot
½ cup meltable candy discs, melted
  (any color you like)
Rock candy in a variety of colors, crushed

Note: *It's much easier to unmold the eggs when they are filled with the ganache and rock candy, instead of unmolding just the shells, so keep them inside the molds until you're all finished!*

1. First, make the ganache. Combine the white chocolate, salt, and whipping cream in a bowl. Place in the freezer until thickened, about 1 hour.

2. Spread some melted candy discs onto the inside of an egg-shaped chocolate mold. Place this in the freezer until the candy has set.

3. Beat the ganache with an electric mixer until it lightens in color and consistency—it should look whipped and hold stiff peaks. Place it into a piping bag fitted with a large, round tip (we suggest the #2D piping tip).

4. Keep the chocolate eggs in the molds and pipe some ganache onto the inside of the eggs.

5. Fill the eggs with rock candy, starting with a dark color in the middle and working outwards into a lighter color.

6. Transfer the eggs to the freezer for the ganache to stiffen, about 30 minutes. Then unmold the eggs and enjoy!

UNICORN FUDGE

This is, without a doubt, the most delicious and addictive fudge you'll ever make! Add your favorite candies and indulge!

4¾ cups good quality white chocolate
1 cup unsalted butter
½ cup corn syrup
1 tsp. vanilla extract
½ cup macadamia nuts
1½ cups rainbow candies (+ extra for topping)
5 cups mini rainbow marshmallows
Cooking spray
Rainbow sprinkles

TIP: *This can be tweaked to suit any season! Change the colors of the candies and sprinkles and swap the vanilla extract for any flavoring you like—peppermint is delicious!*

1. Place the white chocolate, butter, and corn syrup in a pot over medium-low heat. Stir constantly until completely melted. Don't worry if the chocolate and butter separate.

2. Remove from the heat, and stir the mixture with a spatula or a whisk until the chocolate and butter have fully combined. This may take some time, but everything will come together once the mixture slightly cools. Add the vanilla extract and mix to combine. Add the macadamia nuts, rainbow candies, and marshmallows, and mix until just combined.

3. Line a 9x9-inch baking pan with aluminum foil and spray with cooking spray. Pour the mixture into the pan and sprinkle some extra candies and rainbow sprinkles on top. Cover with aluminum foil and place this in the freezer until set.

4. Slice the fudge into bite-sized squares and enjoy!

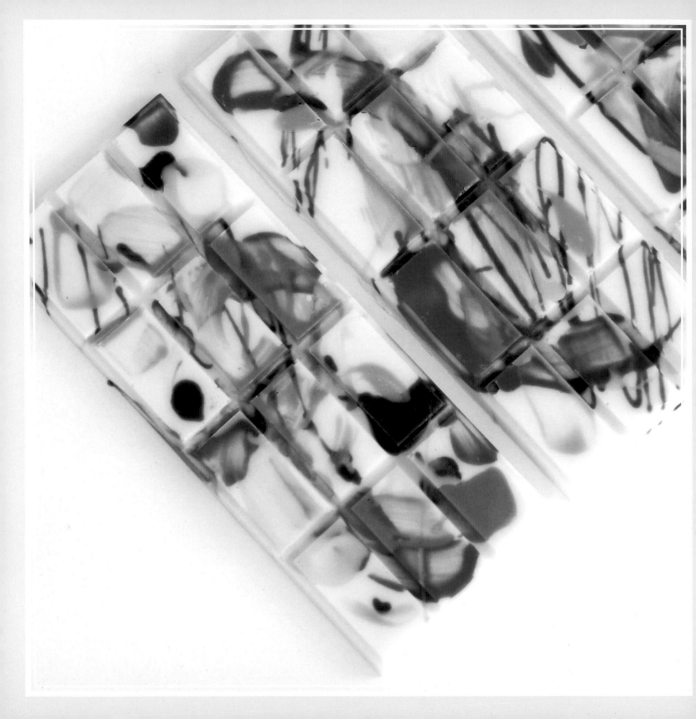

Color Splash Chocolate Bars

Create edible works of art, with a chocolate bar as your canvas!

⅓ cup each of pink, orange, green, blue, and purple meltable candy discs
5 tsp. vegetable shortening, melted
Good quality chocolate (milk, white, or dark), melted

> **TIP:** *Change up the colors of meltable candies to create custom chocolate bars for sporting events, holidays, or birthday parties!*

1. Place the candy discs in individual microwave-safe bowls and microwave at 30-second intervals, until fully melted.

2. Add 1 teaspoon of melted vegetable shortening to each color and mix until well-combined. The vegetable shortening will give a thinner consistency to the melted candy and will help to create a splatter pattern.

3. Drizzle the melted candy discs onto the inside of a chocolate bar mold and create any pattern you like!

4. Place the mold into the fridge until the candy has set.

5. Fill the molds with some melted chocolate and smooth the surface. Place the mold into the freezer until the chocolate has set, about 20 minutes.

6. Unmold the chocolate bars and enjoy!

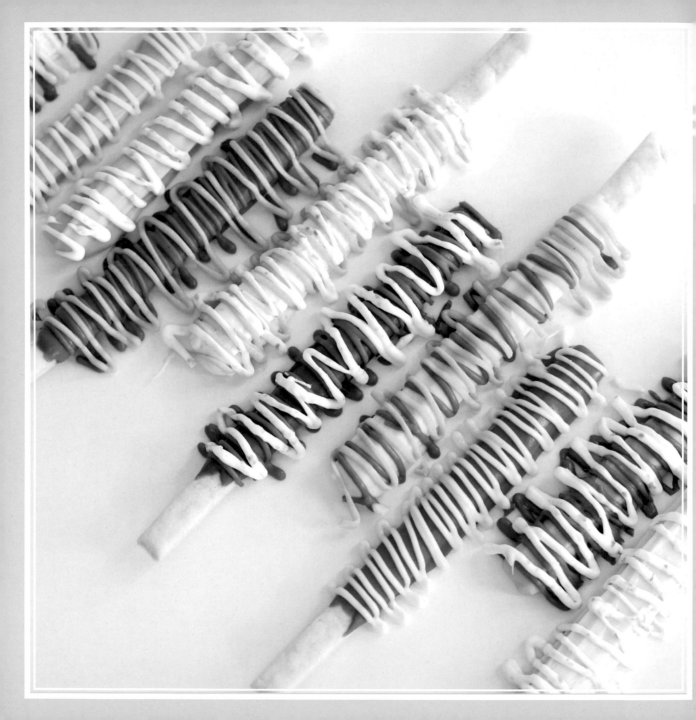

Unicorn To-Go Treats

These are the perfect treat to enjoy on-to-go or keep at work for midday snacking!

½ cup cake flour
½ tbsp. sugar
Pinch of salt
2 tbsp. butter (cold), cut into ½-inch cubes
1½ tbsp. milk
½ tsp. vanilla extract
Pastel meltable candy discs

1. Mix together the cake flour, sugar, and salt in a food processor. Add the cubes of butter and pulse 2–3 times until the butter is well combined. Drizzle the milk and vanilla extract evenly over the mixture. Pulse in the food processor a few more times until the mixture becomes large and crumbly.

2. Shape the dough into a ball and wrap in plastic wrap. Shape it into a disk and set it in the refrigerator for 30 minutes. Once chilled, place on a lightly floured surface and roll the dough out into a 5x 6½-inch rectangle. Slice off the edges to create a clean rectangle.

3. Slice the dough into ¼-inch-wide sticks. Line a baking sheet with parchment paper, and gently transfer the sticks onto the tray by sliding a knife underneath them. Bake them at 350°F for about 10 minutes until they lightly brown. Allow them to slightly cool on the baking sheet, then transfer them to a cooling rack to finish cooling.

4. Melt the candy discs in a microwave-safe bowl for 30-second intervals, until fully melted. Dip the baked sticks into the melted candy and gently run the bottoms of the sticks against the rim of the bowl to remove any excess candy.

5. Place the sticks on a baking sheet lined with parchment paper and allow the candy to set. To speed things up, the baking sheet can be placed in the fridge for the candy to set more quickly. Drizzle a contrasting color of meltable candy on top of the treat sticks. Allow to set and enjoy!

WATERMELON FUDGE

This smooth, creamy watermelon fudge both looks and TASTES like fresh watermelon! Perfect for a summertime picnic.

3 cups granulated sugar
¼ cup unsalted butter
⅔ cup whipping cream
1 tsp. watermelon extract
12 oz. white chocolate chips
7 oz. marshmallow cream
Pink and green food coloring
⅓ cup chocolate chips, to decorate

1. Place the sugar, butter, and cream into a pot and bring to a boil over medium heat, stirring constantly. Once the mixture comes to a boil, boil for an additional 4 minutes, stirring constantly.

2. Remove from the heat and add the watermelon extract and mix well. Add the white chocolate chips and marshmallow cream and mix until fully combined. Divide half of the fudge into 2 small bowls and dye one bowl green. Leave the remaining bowl white. Dye the larger amount of fudge pink.

3. Line an 8-inch round baking dish with aluminum foil and spray with cooking spray. Evenly spread the green fudge into the bottom of the dish. Layer the white, then pink fudge on top. Scatter some chocolate chips onto the surface and gently press down—these will create the seeds!

4. Place the fudge in the freezer for about 45 minutes, until fully set. Slice into watermelon slices and enjoy!

Surprise Chocolate Truffles

Bite into these truffles to reveal a surprise rainbow white chocolate filling!

1¼ cups good quality white chocolate, melted
½ cup whipping cream, heated until hot
Pinch of salt
Red, orange, yellow, green, and blue food
    coloring
1 cup milk chocolate, melted

Make the ganache:

1. Combine the white chocolate, whipping cream, and salt in a bowl. Divide into 5 bowls and dye each a color of the rainbow with food coloring.

2. Place the bowls in the fridge until the ganache is firm, about 1–2 hours.

3. Beat the individual colors with an electric mixer until stiff peaks form. Then place the ganache into piping bags fitted with medium-sized round piping tips. Set aside.

Make the chocolates:

1. Coat the insides of a chocolate mold with some milk chocolate and place it in the freezer until the chocolate has fully set, about 20 minutes. Pipe the ganache into the chocolate shells in the order of the rainbow, then gently smooth the surface with a knife. Pour more chocolate on top, then return the mold to the freezer for the chocolate to set, about 30 minutes.

2. Unmold the chocolates and enjoy!

WHITE CHOCOLATE TARTS

These are the perfect treats for enjoying with tea or for taking to a potluck dinner—they travel very well when popped back into the muffin tin! The white chocolate ganache filling is very smooth and creamy and pairs wonderfully with the vanilla cookie tart shells.

Tart shells:

1 cup flour
Pinch salt
¼ tsp. baking powder
¼ cup unsalted butter, room temperature
½ cup sugar
1 tbsp. milk
½ egg, beaten
½ tsp. vanilla extract
½ cup confetti sprinkles (+ extra for topping)
Cooking spray

White chocolate ganache:

1½ cups good quality white chocolate, melted
½ cup whipping cream, heated until hot
Pinch of salt
Pink, yellow, green, and blue food coloring

Make the tart shells:

1. Mix together the flour, salt, and baking powder in a bowl. In a separate bowl, cream the butter and sugar with an electric mixer until it becomes light and fluffy. Add the milk, egg, and vanilla and mix well. Slowly add the flour mixture until it is just combined. Add the sprinkles and mix until combined.

2. Shape the dough into a ball, then divide it into two balls. Wrap them in plastic wrap and place in the refrigerator for 1 hour.

3. Roll the dough out on a floured surface until it's ⅛ inch thick. Cut out circles with a 4½-inch round cookie cutter. Spray a regular-sized muffin tin with cooking spray. Press the circles into the bottom and sides of the tin. Place the muffin tin in the freezer for 15 minutes for the dough to stiffen.

4. Bake at 350°F for 10 minutes, until the edges are golden. Allow the tarts to fully cool in the pan, then gently remove them from the tin with the tip of a butter knife.

Make the ganache filling:

1. Combine the melted white chocolate, hot whipping cream, and salt in a bowl. Divide the mixture into 4 bowls and dye them pink, yellow, green, and blue.

2. Place the bowls into the fridge until the ganache has stiffened, 1–2 hours.

3. Beat each individual color with an electric mixer until very stiff peaks form.

4. Spread each color of ganache into ¼ of a piping bag fitted with a #2D star-shaped piping tip, so that each color creates a vertical stripe inside the bag.

To assemble:

1. Pipe the ganache into the tarts in a swirling motion.

2. Top with rainbow sprinkles and enjoy!

Chocolate Pudding Terrariums

These are the cutest little desserts! Make 2-3 terrariums, or make mini versions, perfect for use as place settings at a garden party!

Pudding:

¾ cup sugar
½ cup cocoa powder
¼ cup cornstarch
3 cups milk
1 tsp. vanilla extract
1 cup crushed Oreos

Vanilla buttercream:

1 cup unsalted butter, room temperature
½ tsp. vanilla extract
2½ cups confectioner's sugar
Green, yellow, and pink food coloring
Rock candy

Make the pudding:

1. Place the sugar, cocoa powder, and cornstarch in a pot and mix to combine. Gradually add the milk, stirring to combine. Set to low heat and bring to a boil. Boil for 2 minutes, stirring constantly, until thickened.

2. Remove from the heat, pour into a bowl, add the vanilla extract, and stir to combine. Cover the surface with a sheet of plastic wrap and place in the fridge until chilled.

Make the buttercream succulents:

1. Cream the butter with an electric mixer until pale and fluffy. Add the vanilla extract and beat until combined. Add the confectioner's sugar one cup at a time, then beat for 3–5 minutes, until fluffy.

2. Divide the buttercream and dye into a variety of shades of green, yellow, and pink.

3. Spread some buttercream onto the surface of a flower nail (a tool that you use when piping buttercream roses). Place a square of parchment paper on top. Use a variety of piping tips to pipe the succulents of your choice onto the square of buttercream. This recipe used #67, #102, #103, #104, #18, and #2 round tips for the cactus details.

4. Slide the square of parchment paper onto a flat tray and transfer to the freezer until the succulents are very firm.

Assembly:

1. Spoon the chocolate pudding into glasses and top with some crushed Oreos.

2. Gently arrange the succulents inside the glass, then fill in the spaces with rock candy. Enjoy!

TIP: *Freezing the buttercream succulents makes them much easier to handle, and will allow you to easily place them into the glasses without damaging them.*

Marshmallow-Filled Chocolates

These chocolates are filled with a delicious, pillowy vanilla marshmallow filling. They make a wonderful alternative to traditional chocolate truffles!

Pink, yellow, green, blue, and purple meltable candy discs, melted
⅓ cup cold water
2½ tsp. powdered gelatin
1 cup sugar
¼ cup cold water
½ vanilla bean pod (seeds only)

1. Spread your desired shade of melted candy onto the insides of a chocolate mold. Place the mold in the freezer for the chocolate to set.

2. In the meantime, make the marshmallow filling. Pour ⅓ cup of cold water into the bowl of an electric mixer and sprinkle the powdered gelatin on top. Let sit for 5 minutes.

3. Place the sugar and ¼ cup cold water in a small pot and set to medium-high heat. Stir until the sugar has melted.

4. Attach a candy thermometer to the pot and boil the sugar until it reaches 238°F. Brush the sides of the pot with a wet pastry brush if sugar crystals stick to the sides.

5. Add the hot sugar to the gelatin and stir the mixture by hand, whisking for a few minutes to slightly cool. Then beat with an electric mixer on medium-high speed for 8–10 minutes, until soft peaks form. Then add the vanilla bean seeds and mix well.

6. Place the marshmallow into a piping bag fitted with a #12 piping tip and pipe into the chocolate shells. Pour more chocolate on top to seal the marshmallow completely inside the chocolate and return the chocolates to the freezer to set.

7. Unmold the chocolates and enjoy!

RAINBOW CHOCOLATE CHIPS

Create beautiful cookies, cakes, or tarts with these rainbow chocolate chips. Everyone will be asking where you got them!

2 cups white chocolate chips
Oil-based food coloring in rainbow colors
Parchment paper

TIP: *Leaving the chocolate chips to set at room temperature instead of the fridge will prevent the chocolate from "sweating," which can happen when chocolate is transferred into an environment with a different temperature. These can be stored at room temperature and will maintain their shape until you're ready to use them!*

1. Melt the white chocolate chips in the microwave at 30-second intervals.

2. Divide the chocolate into 6 bowls, and dye them pink, orange, yellow, green, blue, and purple, using your oil-based food coloring.

3. Place the parchment paper onto a baking sheet. Using a small spoon, make little dollops of chocolate in each color onto the parchment paper. Allow these to set at room temperature until they have fully hardened, about 24 hours. Then use in whatever recipe you like!

Rainbow Chocolate Eggs

These eggs are so simple to make and would create a beautiful Easter centerpiece or individually packaged as festive snacks!

½ cup each of pink, orange, yellow, green, blue, and purple meltable candy discs, melted

1. Place a dollop of melted pink candy discs into the center of an egg-shaped chocolate mold. Smooth the surface and place the mold in the freezer for the chocolate to set, about 5–10 minutes. Place a dollop of melted orange candy on top and spread it so that the edges reach past the edges of the pink. Return to the freezer to set. Continue in the order of the rainbow until you reach the purple layer.

2. Spread the melted purple candy on top of the blue layer. The purple layer is the last layer, and should fill the remaining space in the molds.

3. Use a knife to flatten the surface of the eggs and remove any extra chocolate—this surface needs to be very flat. Return the mold to the freezer to set, about 10–15 minutes.

4. Unmold the eggs and use the remaining melted purple candy as glue to stick 2 egg halves together, creating a whole egg. Return the chocolates to the freezer once more for the chocolate "glue" to set, about 5 minutes, and enjoy!

RAINBOW CHIP COOKIES

If you're craving chocolate, look no further! These chocolate cookies are wonderfully chewy and taste just like brownies.

3 oz. unsweetened chocolate, chopped
1 cup dark chocolate chips
½ cup unsalted butter, cold and cut into cubes
3 large eggs
1 cup + 2 tbsp. granulated sugar
¾ cup flour
⅓ tsp. baking powder
¼ tsp. salt
¾ cup Rainbow Chocolate Chips (page 187)

1. Place the unsweetened chocolate, dark chocolate chips, and butter into a pot set to medium-low heat, and stir until everything is melted.

2. Place the eggs and sugar in a bowl and whisk on high with an electric mixer until it forms a ribbon when lifted, about 3 minutes.

3. Add the chocolate mixture to the eggs and sugar while whisking. Sift the flour, baking powder, and salt into the bowl and mix just until everything is combined. Then fold in the Rainbow Chocolate Chips.

4. Line a baking sheet with parchment paper and place tablespoon-sized balls of batter about 2 inches apart. Stick some more Rainbow Chocolate Chips on top, and bake at 350°F for 10–12 minutes. Allow the cookies to cool for 1 minute, then transfer them to a cooling rack to cool completely.

Strawberry Chocolate Tarts

These sugar cookie tart shells are filled with a delicious strawberry chocolate ganache. Perfect as a party favor or gift—a single tart for a cute Valentine's Day surprise!

Tart shells:

2 cups flour
¼ tsp. salt
½ tsp. baking powder
½ cup unsalted butter
1 cup sugar
Pink food coloring
2 tbsp. milk
1 large egg
½ tsp. vanilla extract

Ganache filling:

8-oz. strawberry-flavored dark
   chocolate bar
Pinch of salt
¾ cup whipping cream, heated until
   hot

Chocolate hearts:

Melted white chocolate, or meltable
   candy discs in your desired color
Oil-based food coloring (optional, for
   coloring the chocolate)

Whipped cream
Sprinkles, for decorating

Make the tart shells:

1. Mix together the flour, salt, and baking powder in a bowl. In a separate bowl, cream the butter and sugar with an electric mixer until it becomes light and fluffy. Add a couple drops of pink food coloring to the milk, then add that to the mixture along with the egg and vanilla, and mix well. Slowly add the flour mixture until it is just combined.

2. Shape the dough into a ball, then divide it into two balls. Wrap them in plastic wrap and place in the refrigerator for 1 hour.

3. Lightly dust some flour onto your countertop, and roll the dough out until it is ¼ inch thick. Using a 4½-inch circle-shaped cookie cutter, cut out circle shapes.

4. Press the circles into a muffin tin and place in the freezer for 30 minutes, or until frozen solid. Then bake at 350°F for 10 minutes. Allow the tart shells to cool completely in the pan.

5. Gently remove the shells from the pan with the help of a sharp knife. If the shells are a little soft, place them in the freezer to stiffen.

Make the ganache:

1. Break apart the chocolate and place it in a microwave-safe bowl. Microwave at 30-second intervals, stirring at each interval, until fully melted.

2. Add the salt and whipping cream and mix until fully combined. Place in the fridge until chilled, but still liquid.

continued on page 194

3. Pour the ganache into the tarts and place in the fridge until the ganache is firm.

Make the chocolate hearts:

1. Dye the white chocolate your desired color with oil-based food coloring, or use colored candy discs.

2. Pour the chocolate into a heart-shaped chocolate mold and place in the freezer until the chocolate has fully set, about 20 minutes.

3. Unmold the chocolates and keep them in the freezer until needed.

Assembly:

1. Place a dollop of whipped cream onto the center of each tart. Top with a chocolate heart and sprinkles. Enjoy!

TIP: *You can substitute the strawberry chocolate bar in the ganache for any flavor chocolate bar you like! Orange chocolate, mint chocolate, or cookies and cream chocolate would be delicious.*

Acknowledgments

Writing a cookbook has been a dream of mine ever since I started my YouTube channel. I still remember every little detail of the day I received the email from my editor at Skyhorse Publishing, asking if I had ever thought about writing a cookbook. Amidst my jumping and screaming for joy, it took all of me not to just reply, "YES, YES, YES, THIS IS MY ABSOLUTE DREAM!!!"

This is a milestone that I didn't dare let myself dream about at this stage in my career. I believed it would be years before this opportunity would arise and didn't want to get my hopes up too soon. But thanks to Leah Zarra, this experience has been everything I thought it would be, and so much more. I was given so much creative freedom from choosing the recipes, collaborating on the layout and cover of the book, as well as all my own photography. I had to pinch myself multiple times in my studio, whispering to myself, "You're taking photos for your *book*. These are going to be printed and bound and seen by people you've never met." It was so humbling and exciting. There were many days that I was awake until 4:00 a.m. working on this book, but it was absolutely worth it.

The amazing team at Skyhorse Publishing, especially Leah, made me feel so comfortable and supported me during this entire journey, and I cannot thank them enough. Thank you to Nicole Frail for discovering my recipes, and to Skyhorse for having faith in me. I am so incredibly lucky and cannot believe that I've been blessed with such an opportunity so early into my career.

Another thank you goes out to my subscribers and followers on YouTube, Instagram, and Facebook. To put it simply, I would not be here if it was not for you. Your love, support, and enthusiasm for my content has given me the opportunity to have the life and career I've always dreamed of. I cherish every single view, comment, and like, and will never take any of it for granted. The family that we've created is so fun-loving and happy, and I'm so excited to hear what you think of this book. I look forward to many more years of recipes, livestreams, and foodie fun with every single one of you. You are amazing and have given me a life of purpose and rainbows. Thank you all so much, I love you! This book is for you.

I also want to thank my family. They have been unconditionally supportive since I started my YouTube channel. They've been there when I struggled with paying bills and have celebrated with me when new opportunities arose. They are my cheerleaders when I lose faith in myself and have been with me every step of the way. I would not be the person I am today without them. I have never felt judged or pressured to be anything other than my true self and I feel incredibly lucky to have the best parents anyone could have asked for. Mom and Dad, thank you so much for raising me and giving me the confidence in myself to pursue my dreams.

And last but not least, thank you to the person who is reading this. Whether you have purchased it, received as a gift, or are browsing through it at the bookstore, thank you for taking the time to pick up my book and flip through it. I sincerely hope it does not disappoint!

INDEX

CONVERSION CHARTS

METRIC AND IMPERIAL CONVERSIONS

(These conversions are rounded for convenience)

Ingredient	Cups/Tablespoons/Teaspoons	Ounces	Grams/Milliliters
Butter	1 cup/16 tablespoons/2 sticks	8 ounces	230 grams
Cheese, shredded	1 cup	4 ounces	110 grams
Cream cheese	1 tablespoon	0.5 ounce	14.5 grams
Cornstarch	1 tablespoon	0.3 ounce	8 grams
Flour, all-purpose	1 cup/1 tablespoon	4.5 ounces/0.3 ounce	125 grams/8 grams
Flour, whole wheat	1 cup	4 ounces	120 grams
Fruit, dried	1 cup	4 ounces	120 grams
Fruits or veggies, chopped	1 cup	5 to 7 ounces	145 to 200 grams
Fruits or veggies, puréed	1 cup	8.5 ounces	245 grams
Honey, maple syrup, or corn syrup	1 tablespoon	0.75 ounce	20 grams
Liquids: cream, milk, water, or juice	1 cup	8 fluid ounces	240 milliliters
Oats	1 cup	5.5 ounces	150 grams
Salt	1 teaspoon	0.2 ounces	6 grams
Spices: cinnamon, cloves, ginger, or nutmeg (ground)	1 teaspoon	0.2 ounce	5 milliliters
Sugar, brown, firmly packed	1 cup	7 ounces	200 grams
Sugar, white	1 cup/1 tablespoon	7 ounces/0.5 ounce	200 grams/12.5 grams
Vanilla extract	1 teaspoon	0.2 ounce	4 grams

OVEN TEMPERATURES

Fahrenheit	Celsius	Gas Mark
225°	110°	¼
250°	120°	½
275°	140°	1
300°	150°	2
325°	160°	3
350°	180°	4
375°	190°	5
400°	200°	6
425°	220°	7
450°	230°	8